The Filmgoer's Book of Quotes

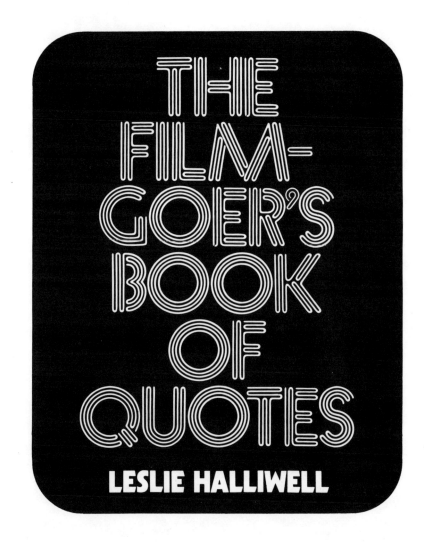

THE FILM-GOER'S BOOK OF QUOTES

LESLIE HALLIWELL

ARLINGTON HOUSE·PUBLISHERS

NEW ROCHELLE, N. Y.

Granada Publishing Limited
First published in Great Britain 1973 by Hart-Davis, MacGibbon Ltd
Frogmore, St Albans, Hertfordshire AL2 2NF, and
3 Upper James Street, London W1R 4BP

MANUFACTURED IN THE UNITED STATES OF AMERICA

Library of Congress Cataloging in Publication Data

Halliwell, Leslie, comp.
    The filmgoer's book of quotes.

    1. Moving-pictures—Anecdotes, facetiae, satire,
etc. 2. Moving-pictures—Quotations, maxims, etc.
3. Moving-pictures—Miscellanea. I. Title.
PN1994.9.H3 1974   791.43'02'07   74-6224
ISBN 0-8700-285-6

This book
is for
RUTH

Contents

Foreword

When recollected in tranquillity, the pleasure a movie gives is often best expressed by the good characteristic bits of dialogue one remembers. If we wrote them down at the time we would amass a huge encyclopaedia of emotion and wit, phrased as pithily as talent, sophistication and high salaries can induce.

As well as what they write and say *in* the movies, show biz people are always talking *about* the movies. Their talk can be succinct, constructive, envious, enthusiastic or just plain bitchy: it adds up to a bird's eye view of the seventh art, an art that is also an industry whose products are tears and laughter.

This is a small compilation of memorable movie quotes. They come from an immense variety of sources, hardly any from my personal experience. I can however claim to be the only person who overheard a splendid ad lib by A. E. Matthews. In 1957, when Matty was nearly ninety, he was invited among a selection of top British film talent to a mammoth party at Pinewood Studios to celebrate twenty-one years of film production there. Lunch was provided in a huge marquee, and afterwards several top table guests got up to speak. Kenneth More and Jack Hawkins were witty and brief, but there followed a halting forty-minute ramble from Sir Leonard Brockington, who seemed rather incredibly to be talking about the spirit of man: what this had to do with a film studio party was not clear. Matty drank his port happily enough for a while, and then took to toying impatiently with the cutlery. After twenty-five minutes or so of unallayed boredom, Sir Leonard made a significant pause, and some people, thinking he had finished, began to applaud, an act in which Matty enthusiastically joined. When the applause died down and Sir Leonard doggedly continued, Matty groaned. 'Good God,' he said in a very audible undertone, 'Doesn't he know I haven't got long to live?'

When I think back on forty years of filmgoing, the oddest fragments of dialogue float into my consciousness. There is Ernest Thesiger as the nervous Horace Femm in *The Old Dark House*, welcoming his guests with:

Have some gin...it's my only weakness...

There is cross-eyed Ben Turpin, who in his heyday was difficult to handle because he was over-impressed by his own star status and inflated salary. According to Mack Sennett he used to enter public places and announce himself as follows:

Ben Turpin! Three thousand dollars a week!

There is that executive command after a stormy interview, variously attributed to Jack Warner, Darryl Zanuck and Sam Goldwyn:

Never let that son of a bitch in the studio again...
until we need him.

There is a splendid sub-title from the silent *King of Kings*, in which the Queen of Sheba springs into action and commands:

Harness my zebras, gift of the Nubian King!

There are the ads for the early musicals, which for a while were billed as

100% talking! 100% singing! 100% dancing!

which must have added up to three hundred per cent of something. There is Butch the bulldog in a Tom and Jerry cartoon. In a Brooklynesque voice which seems to belong to Jimmy Durante, he enunciates as follows to his infant son:

First, you gotta loin to chase cats...which happens
to be my specialty!

(The upward inflection of that last phrase is what really makes me laugh.) The same Butch, at the end of the cartoon, proudly surveys his infant barking up a tree at the terrified Tom, and explains to a passerby:

Dat's ma boy, over dere, doing dat!

Yes, cartoon characters gave me a lot of fun, and none more than Sylvester the lisping cat, who at the start of one film addressed Tweety Pie the canary in friendly but frank manner:

Hello, breakfatht!

On another occasion, when Sylvester is battered and befuddled after five minutes of vain but violent attempts to catch the bird, he despairingly says to the audience:

There mutht be thome eathier way for a puthy cat to get thome thuthtenanthe...

A quotable quote about the movies, as about any other subject, expresses far more than the immediate joke. Something once said by Steve Broidy, President of Monogram, tells quite a lot about B picture making and exploitation in the old days. Broidy was shown a glossy press book for one of his current efforts, to which the superlatives in the copy bore little relation. After examining the blurbs for a while, he grinned and said:

Why don't we put sprocket holes on the press book and throw the picture away?

Dinah Shore summed up the appeal of a certain type of star when she said:

Bing Crosby sings like all people think *they sing in the shower.*

Sir Cedric Hardwicke hinted at the unconsidered difficulties of an actor's life:

I suffer from what used to be called Sir tax. A knighthood inflates the cost of living beyond belief.

Billie Burke hauntingly expressed the fear of every ageing actress:

Ah, that sad and bewildering moment when you are no longer the cherished darling, but must turn the corner and try to be funny.

Christopher Lee, on the defensive in 1960, unwittingly predicted the descending spiral of public taste:

In The Mummy *I only kill three people – and not in a ghastly way. I just break their necks.*

When he spoke in 1935 of Shirley Temple, Franklin D. Roosevelt capsuled the social effect of the movies:

During this depression, when the spirit of the people is lower than at any other time, it is a splendid thing that for just fifteen cents an American can go to a movie and look at the smiling face of a baby and forget his troubles.

The purpose of this book, then, is not entirely frivolous. A fun book it certainly aims to be, but it should also provide a useful source for those who need to know about movies, to write about them, or simply to be well-informed about an aspect of the way we live in the twentieth century. It naturally makes no claim to be comprehensive: the selection is mine. There are no lengthy excerpts from speeches: almost all the quotations are brief expressions of an attitude, stated with wit or what passes for wit.

The quotations are arranged in arbitrary fashion. A few important people or subjects have short sections to themselves; others are arranged in quiz form under subjects. The purpose of the quizzes is to provide a little extra entertainment; but the answers follow at once. Finally, there is an index of speakers and their targets.

As in the case of *The Filmgoer's Companion*, to which this

hopes to provide an amiable appendage, any corrections or additions will be more than welcome, and should be addressed to me care of the publishers.

L.H.
March 1973

ACKNOWLEDGEMENTS and thanks are due to all those whose wit and wisdom have unwittingly helped to build up this book: the actors in interview, the wandering journalists, the writers of books and scripts, and perhaps above all the producers and directors who made Hollywood what it used to be, and is no more.

THE DECORATIONS are a selection of original press advertisements which it is hoped that the reader will find amusing and nostalgic, deriving as they do from the first few years of talking pictures. To the creative artists who designed these and many thousands of other advertisements, my humble and sincere thanks for a lifetime of quiet pleasure and amusement. To MCA, who now control Paramount's older films, my thanks for permission to reproduce these fragments of social history.

Bud Abbott (1895-) and Lou Costello (1906-59)

Abbott and Costello flourished in the forties. They were fast-talking, empty-headed slapstick comedians who depended on caricature and contrast: the fat and the thin, the nervous and the foolhardy, the stupid and the stupider. Their work falls into well-remembered routines and reactions. There is chubby, terrified Costello calling after his partner:

Ch-ch-ch-ch-ch-i-ck!

There is his shy admission:

I'm a ba-a-a-ad boy!

There is the old pantomime gag of his seeing something alarming and running to tell his partner; by the time the latter returns the thing has naturally disappeared. There are repetitive routines such as the 'Slowly I turned' scene from *Lost in a Harem*, with its Laurel and Hardy-like inevitability. Most memorably there is skilful nightclub crosstalk, seen at its best in the 'Who's on first' sketch which first brought them to fame and which they filmed in *One Night in the Tropics* and *The Naughty Nineties*. Here is part of it:

> *A: You know, these days they give ballplayers very peculiar names. Take the St Louis team: Who's on first, What's on second, I Don't Know is on third...*
> *C: That's what I want to find out. I want you to tell me the names of the fellows on the St Louis team.*
> *I'm telling you. Who's on first, What's on second, I Don't Know is on third.*
> *— Who's playing first?*
> *Yes.*

1

— I mean, the fellow's name on first base.
Who.
— The fellow playing first base.
Who.
— The guy on first base.
Who is on first.
— Well, what are you asking me for?
I'm not asking you, I'm telling you. Who is on first.
— I'm asking you — who is on first?
That's the man's name.
— That's who's name?
Yes.
— Well, go ahead tell me.
Who!
— All I'm trying to find out is, what's the guy's name on first base.
Oh no, What is on second.
— I'm not asking you who's on second.
Who's on first.
— That's what I'm trying to find out! What's the guy's name on first base?
What's the guy's name on second base.
— I'm not asking who's on second.
Who's on first.
— I Don't Know.
He's on third...

And so on, for another five minutes.

Actors
and Acting

A short selection of attitudes.

George Sanders:

> *Acting is like roller skating. Once you know how to do it, it is neither stimulating nor exciting.*

Anthony Quinn:

> *In Europe an actor is an artist. In Hollywood, if he isn't working, he's a bum.*

Alfred Lunt:

> *The secret of my success? I speak in a loud clear voice and try not to bump into the furniture.*

Ethel Barrymore:

> *We who play, who entertain for a few years, what can we leave that will last?*

Marlon Brando:

> *Acting is the expression of a neurotic impulse.*
>
> *Acting is a bum's life. Quitting acting, that is the sign of maturity.*

Alfred Hitchcock:

> *Actors are cattle.*

NB. When attacked for this remark Hitch claimed he had been

misquoted: what he really said was: 'Actors should be *treated* like cattle.'

Charles Chaplin:

> *Film acting is unquestionably a director's medium.*

NB. Chaplin used to advise his silent actors: 'Don't sell it. Remember they're *peeking* at you.'

Dorothy Parker:

> *Scratch an actor – and you'll find an actress.*

Paul Newman:

> *Acting is a question of absorbing other people's personalities and adding some of your own experience.*

Claude Rains:

> *I learn the lines and pray to God.*

Alternative Titles

Quiz

A few films over the years have been advertised with alternative secondary titles, usually connected by the word 'or'.
By what main titles are these films better known?

1 *The Eighth Wonder of the World*
2 *The Shame of a Nation*
3 *The Diary of an Innocent Young Man*
4 *Love's Struggle Through the Ages*
5 *Pardon me, but your Teeth are in my Neck*
6 *Where were you the Night you said you shot down Baron Von Richthofen?*
7 *How to Stop Worrying and Love the Bomb*
8 *How I Flew from London to Paris in 25 Hours 11 Minutes*
9 *How to make a French Dish*
10 *A Story of the London Fog*
11 *Ten Weeks with a Circus*
12 *A Love Story*

1 Said to be one of the few points contributed to *King Kong* by Edgar Wallace, who went to Hollywood in 1931 to work on the film but died before it was completed.

2 When Howard Hughes made *Scarface* in 1932 it was attacked as a glorification of the Al Capones of America. He therefore added this extra title to show where the film's sympathies officially lay, and even offered to make it the main title; but this never happened.

3 *Benjamin*, the 1968 French attempt to out-dare *Tom Jones*.

4 D. W. Griffith's *Intolerance* (1915). The sub-title was added to make it sound more attractive to the general public, but it failed disastrously.

5 *The Fearless Vampire Killers* (1969), released in Britain as *Dance of the Vampires*. The sub-title indicates the kind of humour aimed at (but certainly not achieved).

6 *Darling Lili* (1969). Although widely mentioned during production, the alternative title was not used on release.

7 *Dr Strangelove* (1963). As one might have expected, the film did not provide the remedy it offered.

8 *Those Magnificent Men in their Flying Machines* (1965). The two titles together must form the longest billing in history.

9 *La Bonne Soupe* (1964). An amiable pun which did not help the film at the box office.

10 Hitchcock's *The Lodger* (1926).

11 Walt Disney's *Toby Tyler* (1964).

12 *Intermezzo* (1939).

Julie
Andrews (1934-   )

This English young lady who conquered America in *My Fair Lady* on Broadway, and went on to win an Academy Award for her first film *Mary Poppins* (1964), is interesting as the movies' last throwback to the kind of star they were creating in gentler times, and as an example of how quickly the biggest star can fall out of fashion in the restless seventies. One senses that she is realistic enough to have enjoyed the good times while they lasted, and to fall from grace gracefully. But she may fight. After *The Sound of Music*, Christopher Plummer said that:

> *Working with her is like being hit over the head with a Valentine's card.*

and some anonymous gentleman described her as:

> *Like a nun with a switchblade.*

Moss Hart said:

> *She has that wonderful British strength that makes you wonder why they lost India.*

Miss Andrews does seem to merit the suggestion of steel beneath the velvet. When she accepted her Oscar, which many thought went to her out of sympathy because Warners refused her the film of *My Fair Lady*, her little speech ran:

> *I'd like to thank all those who made this possible — especially Jack Warner.*

Having got to the top by being sweet and old-fashioned, she quickly showed signs of disliking her own image.

7

I don't want to be thought of as wholesome,

she said in 1966, and promptly proved it by accepting a sexy role. She was also seen wearing a badge which read:

Mary Poppins is a junkie.

But her serene self-confidence may be something of a sham. She once said:

Films are much more my level. On stage I never feel quite enough...

One way or another, she achieved, briefly, a worldwide image best expressed by a *Time* magazine interviewer:

She's everybody's tomboy tennis partner and their daughter, their sister, their mum...She is Christmas carols in the snow, a companion by the fire, a laughing clown at charades, a girl to read poetry to on a cold winter's night...

The Animal Kingdom

Movie title makers often use animal allusions because they are vivid and picturesque (though not always meaningful to the viewer). Can you supply the animals missing from the following titles?

1 .... *Seed*
2 *Cry* ....
3 *The Fallen* ....
4 *A Gathering of* ....
5 *Flying* ....
6 *After the* ....
7 *Poor* ....
8 *Brother* ....
9 .... *Feathers*
10 *The* ....'s *Stratagem*
11 *The* .... *Trap*
12 *Track of the* ....
13 *The Flight of the* ....
14 *The Sleeping* ....
15 *Dear* ....
16 *Straw* ....
17 *Madame* ....
18 .... *Squadron*
19 *The Voice of the* ....
20 .... *Woman*

1 *Dragon Seed*
2 *Cry Wolf*
3 *The Fallen Sparrow*
4 *A Gathering of Eagles*
5 *Flying Elephants* (Laurel and Hardy) or *Flying Tigers* (John Wayne)
6 *After the Fox*
7 *Poor Cow*
8 *Brother Rat*
9 *Horse Feathers*
10 *The Spider's Stratagem*
11 *The Rabbit Trap*
12 *Track of the Cat*
13 *The Flight of the Phoenix*
14 *The Sleeping Tiger*
15 *Dear Octopus*
16 *Straw Dogs*
17 *Madame Butterfly*
18 *Eagle Squadron* or *Dragonfly Squadron*
19 *The Voice of the Turtle*
20 Women being all things to all men, a wide choice is possible: *Snake Woman, Cobra Woman, Spider Woman, Wasp Woman* etc.

Fred
Astaire (1899-)

The most famous quote about the screen's nimblest dancer is the report of the studio talent scout on his first screen test:

> *Can't act. Can't sing. Slightly bald. Can dance a little.*

In later years, when he was a household name around the world, he tried to match that for humility:

> *I have no desire to prove anything by dancing. I have never used it as an outlet or as a means of expressing myself. I just dance.*

And:

> *I just put my feet in the air and move them around.*

But in another mood, he did once confess:

> *I suppose I made it look easy, but gee whiz, did I work and worry.*

Gene Kelly summed up his appeal:

> *He can give the audience pleasure just by walking across the floor.*

Bad
Guys

What wicked (but fascinating) characters spoke these lines, and
in what films?

1 First the hunt, then the revels!
2 We'll start with a few murders. Big men. Little men. Just
  to show we make no distinction.
3 Some people are better off dead. Like your wife and my
  father, for instance.
4 A soul? A soul is nothing. Can you see it? Smell it? Touch
  it? No…
5 Listen to them: children of the night. What music they
  make…
6 Synthetic flesh! Synthetic flesh!
7 I say, marriage with Max is not exactly a bed of roses, is it?
8 Mother of mercy, is this the end of Rico?
9 In Italy for thirty years under the Borgias they had
  warfare, terror, murder, bloodshed – they produced
  Michelangelo, Leonardo da Vinci, and the Renaissance. In
  Switzerland they had brotherly love, five hundred years of
  democracy and peace, and what did that produce? The
  cuckoo clock.
10 The world shall hear from me again…
11 I distrust a man that says when. If he's got to be careful
   not to drink too much it's because he's not to be trusted
   when he does.
And a few bad gals:
12 You have nothing to stay for. You have nothing to live for,
   really, have you? Look down there – it's easy, isn't it?
13 Gimme visky…ginger ale on the side. And don't be stingy,
   baby.
14 It took more than one man to change my name to Shanghai
   Lily.

Answers

1 Count Zaroff (Leslie Banks) in *The Most Dangerous Game* (1932), sometimes known as *The Hounds of Zaroff*. Zaroff is a rich villain who lures men to his island in order to hunt them, and keeps a trophy room of human heads. Needless to say, Joel McCrea outwits him.

2 Claude Rains as *The Invisible Man* (1933). Griffin has been turned by the power of his invisibility drugs into a raving megalomaniac.

3 Robert Walker as Bruno Anthony explaining to Guy Haines (Farley Granger) his plan for swapping murders at the outset of Hitchcock's *Strangers on a Train* (1951).

4 One can almost hear Walter Huston relishing these lines from *All that Money can Buy* (1941). In this New Hampshire version of *Faust* he played the devil, or Mr Scratch as he was locally known. James Craig was the easily persuaded victim.

5 The voice has been imitated a million times, but only Bela Lugosi, as *Dracula* (1930) could extract the chilling essence from these simple lines.

6 Very difficult! Preston Foster as the mad doctor in the preposterous finale of *Doctor X* (1932). Having appeared to be the only character who cannot be the strangler, because he has only one arm, he is seen in his laboratory rapidly growing another by the application of the compound to which he refers.

7 Inimitably spoken by George Sanders as the caddish cousin Jack Favell in *Rebecca* (1940).

8 One of the most famous lines in movies: Edward G. Robinson expiring at the end of *Little Caesar* (1930).

9 And one of the most famous speeches, written by Orson Welles to extend his tiny role as Harry Lime in *The Third Man* (1949). It ends the famous Ferris wheel scene in which he defends his black market activities.

10 The yellow peril, Fu Manchu, played by Christopher Lee in *The Face of Fu Manchu* (1965).

11 Sidney Greenstreet as 'the fat man', Gutman, in *The Maltese Falcon* (1941): a rich and memorable portrayal of an oily but estimable villain.

12 *Rebecca* again, but this time the dark housekeeper Mrs Danvers, played by Judith Anderson; here she tries to persuade the second Mrs de Winter to commit suicide.

13 A well-remembered line because it was the first to be spoken on the screen by Greta Garbo, as the waterfront tramp in *Anna Christie* (1931).

14 An unspeakable line, one would think, but at the beginning of *Shanghai Express* (1932) Marlene Dietrich still gets away with it.

Tallulah
Bankhead (1902-68)

What one remembers about Miss Bankhead is not her merit as a performer, which in her heyday was considerable, but rather her well-publicised life style, which kept her in the headlines throughout the twenties and thirties. As Mrs Patrick Campbell said:

> *Tallulah is always skating on thin ice. Everyone wants to be there when it breaks.*

The lady herself issued such statements as:

> *Cocaine isn't habit-forming. I should know – I've been using it for years.*

As a result, in her later years:

> *They used to photograph Shirley Temple through gauze. They should photograph me through linoleum.*

But it was more sad than funny when someone asked:

> *Are you really the famous Tallulah?*

and got the answer:

> *What's left of her.*

John
Barrymore (1882-1942)

Barrymore was forty-four when he finally moved to Hollywood and gave up the stage. His 'great profile' still had years of use. Said Heywood Broun:

> *He moved through a movie scene like an exquisite paper knife.*

He was a match for co-stars like Katharine Hepburn, who at the end of shooting of *A Bill of Divorcement* said:

> *Thank goodness I don't have to act with you any more.*

He cooed in reply:

> *I didn't know you ever had, darling.*

For several years he maintained the bravura of an actor who had once flung a fish at a coughing audience and cried:

> *Busy yourselves with that, you damned walruses, while the rest of us proceed with the play!*

But dissipation hastened his twilight years. He looked into the dressing room mirror one day and said:

> *I'm fifty years old and I want to look like Jackie Cooper's grandson.*

Basically he began to fear and despise the cinema:

> *If you stay in front of that camera long enough, it*

*will show you not only what you had for breakfast
but who your ancestors were.*

His last illnesses occupied several years, but his constitution was remarkable and his spirit defiant :

> *Die? I should say not, old fellow. No Barrymore
> would allow such a conventional thing to happen to
> him.*

1932

Humphrey Bogart (1899-1957)

To some extent Bogart tended to live his film roles. As Dave Chasen the Hollywood restaurateur once said:

> *Bogart's a helluva nice guy till 11.30 p.m. After that he thinks he's Bogart.*

So in a way his aptest quotes are from his movies. As Rick in *Casablanca*:

> *I stick my neck out for nobody.*

Or as Sam Spade in *The Maltese Falcon*:

> *Don't be so sure I'm as crooked as I'm supposed to be.*

And:

> *When you're slapped, you'll take it and like it!*

Stanley Kramer saw through him:

> *He was playing Bogart all the time, but he was really just a big sloppy bowl of mush.*

One feels that this hits the nail pretty squarely on the head: Bogie was a nice guy who enjoyed a good grouch. About, for instance, the untrained beefcake stars of the early fifties, many of them picked up for tests from sidewalks and gas stations:

> *Shout 'gas' around the studios today, and half the young male stars will come running.*

About acting theorists:

> *Do I subscribe to the Olivier school of acting? Ah, nuts. I'm an actor. I just do what comes naturally.*

About the industry:

> *I don't hurt the industry. The industry hurts itself, by making so many lousy movies — as if General Motors deliberately put out a bad car.*

About his innumerable gangster roles before his rise to star status:

> *I was always the guy behind the guy behind the gun.*

About middle age:

> *The hell with the hair on your head. It's the hair on your chest that counts.*

He needn't have worried. John Crosby said:

> *Off screen, he didn't diminish.*

And he summed himself up with accuracy and satisfaction:

> *I'm a professional. I've done pretty well, don't you think? I've survived in a pretty rough business.*

Censorship

The bounds of permissibility have troubled the film industry since Fatima's belly dance in 1897. Each country developed its own set of rules, generally based on American feeling, which after the advent of talkies became notably less stringent until the Legion of Decency cracked down in 1934. There followed thirty years of absurdity, but during the sixties the fetters were somewhat too abruptly removed. Bob Hope's wisecracks were a pointer to the changing times. In 1962 he said:

> *Nowadays when a film is awarded the Production Code seal the producer cries: 'Where have we failed?'*

And in 1965:

> *They are doing things on the screen now that I wouldn't do in bed. If I could.*

And in 1970:

> *They are doing things on the screen these days that the French don't even put on postcards.*

As the British censor John Trevelyan said in 1970:

> *The Americans are nice people but right now they're behaving like small boys who've just discovered what sex is.*

Ten years earlier he had defended his calling:

We are paid to have dirty minds.

In the fifties, Robert Rossen summed up most people's attitude to censorship:

I don't like it, but nor do I like the absence of it.

Joseph Wood Krutch thought that:

The inanities blessed by the Hays Office are more genuinely corrupting than any pornography.

Jean Renoir was cynically accurate:

It is in the interest of producers to maintain a certain moral standard since, if they don't do this, the immoral films won't sell.

There was bound to be a backlash after so many years of utterly ridiculous censorial attitudes. Consider the famous remark by the Chicago Chief of Police in the thirties:

Any film that isn't fit to be shown to my youngest child isn't fit to be shown to anybody.

As a result of such attitudes, an anonymous wag remarked:

Hollywood buys a good story about a bad girl and has to change it to a bad story about a good girl.

Fritz Lang recalled that when shooting *Man Hunt* in 1940

The Hays Office warned us that we couldn't show the heroine as a prostitute. We had to put a sewing machine in her apartment, so in that way she was not a whore but a seamstress.

Here is a partial list of themes banned by the British Board of Film Censors in the early thirties:

travesties of religious rites
references to royalty
hangings or executions either serious or comic
political propaganda
too much shooting
intoxication
cruelty
companionate marriage
free love
immodesty
vamping
vulgar noises
harsh screams
the divinity
life after death
British officers shown in an unflattering light

It seems surprising that any films were made at all. Around the same time, the BBFC made its sublime public announcement about its reasons for banning Germaine Dulac's *The Seashell and the Clergyman*:

> *This film is apparently meaningless. If there is any meaning it is doubtless objectionable.*

And in 1936 Lord Tyrrell, the Board's head, stated that:

> *The cinema needs continual repression of controversy to stave off disaster.*

The makers of *Gone with the Wind* in 1939 had trouble with two of Rhett Butler's lines. They finally got acceptance for:

> *Frankly, my dear, I don't give a damn.*

But the censors refused to allow:

> *I've never held fidelity to be a virtue.*

During the same year, a script for *Zaza* involved the heroine

screaming at the villain: 'Pig! Pig! Pig! Pig! Pig!' Back
came a note from the censor's office:

Delete two pigs.

In *Destry Rides Again*, Marlene Dietrich was allowed to tuck
money down her bosom, but her following remark was deleted:

There's gold in them thar hills.

This reminds one of Marilyn Monroe's later remark:

*The trouble with censors is they worry if a girl has
cleavage. They ought to worry if she hasn't any.*

In the long run, there are always ways of getting round censorship, at least for knowing audiences. When Charles Laughton
was told he could not show the incestuous side of Edward
Moulton-Barrett he said:

They can't censor the gleam in my eye.

And as Lord Eccles, Minister of the Arts, said in 1972:

*The only censor is the audience, which will decide
whether it wants it and how soon it gets fed up
with it.*

Charles
Chaplin (1889-)

The son of a bitch is a ballet dancer!

So pronounced W. C. Fields, having been urged to sit
through and enjoy a Chaplin movie. Fields promptly realized
that the Chaplin brand of comic art was not only more popular
than his own, but one which it was impossible for him to emu-
late. He continued:

> *He's the best ballet dancer that ever lived, and if I
> get a good chance I'll strangle him with my bare
> hands...*

Many people have been jealous of Chaplin's success, partly
because he was never modest about it. His poverty-stricken
childhood made him mercenary, and once at the top he dis-
played a private personality it was difficult to like. Even his
friend Mary Pickford called him:

> *That obstinate, suspicious, egocentric, maddening
> and loveable genius of a problem child.*

And Chaplin has never found a way of making friends with
his public. Even in his autobiography he seems at pains to
present himself unsympathetically, as when he recalls telling
Mack Sennett:

> *The public doesn't line up outside the box office
> when your name appears as they do for mine.*

His memories of his manifold romantic activities are tastelessly
presented:

> *Like everyone else's, my sex-life went in circles.
> Sometimes I was potent, other times disappointing.*

In the more intimate details his phrasing is curious to say the least:

> *(She was) a big handsome woman of twenty-two,*
> *well built, with upper regional domes immensely*
> *expansive and made alluring by an extremely low*
> *decolleté summer dress which, on the drive home,*
> *evoked my libidinous curiosity...*

His willingness to prognosticate on matters of which he plainly knows little, such as the true authorship of the Shakespeare plays, is often foolhardy:

> *I can hardly think it was the Stratford boy. Who-*
> *ever wrote them had an aristocratic personality.*

His philosophy is usually naïve, as in his much-attacked de-fence of murder in *Monsieur Verdoux*:

> *Wars, conflict, it's all business. One murder makes*
> *a villain. Millions, a hero. Numbers sanctify...*

Determined to make his clown a tragic hero, he is frequently guilty of relentless sentimentality. The opening title of *The Kid* runs:

> *A picture with a smile and perhaps a tear.*

As Hannen Swaffer once said:

> *His gospel is like Mary Pickford's: the hope of a*
> *little child.*

Billy Wilder was more caustic:

> *When he found a voice to say what was on his*
> *mind, he was like a child of eight writing lyrics for*
> *Beethoven's Ninth.*

He frequently over-estimates himself. Of *The Great Dictator* he declared:

25

I made this picture for the Jews of the world.

He is a poor loser. Having been forced to leave the United States, which made him rich and to which he owed a large amount in back taxes, he stated :

I have no further use for America. I wouldn't go back there if Jesus Christ was President.

Over the years he has alternately denied and proclaimed his Jewishness. This was a typical announcement of the late forties:

I am not a Jew! I am a citizen of the world! I am not a communist! I am a peacemonger!

A rather limited attitude is struck in his remark about Negroes:

They have suffered too much ever to be funny to me.

(Yet Chaplin's own comedy derives from poverty and deprivation.) He has taken credit for every aspect of his films, and frequently denied it to those who helped him most. Yet he is not an inventive director:

I am the unusual and do not need camera angles.

Cinematographer Karl Struss said of him:

He has no knowledge of camera direction. His films are completely theatre.

Yet there is no denying that Chaplin managed very well by feeding his own self-importance. He used to say:

You have to believe in yourself, that's the secret.

And as late as 1960:

I remain one thing and one thing only, and that is

a clown. It places me on a far higher plane than
any politician.

In a sense he is right. Despite all Chaplin's failings, his tramp is an archetypal creation which strikes a chord in everybody and will live as long as films can be preserved. Chaplin always knew the virtue of simplicity:

All I need to make a comedy is a park, a policeman
and a pretty girl.

That was in 1916, and ambition soon overtook him. Colleen Moore in her autobiography *Silent Star* tells that in 1922 a producer was contemplating a life of Christ, and Chaplin demanded audience and became very excited:

I want to play the role of Jesus. I'm a logical choice.
I look the part. I'm a Jew. And I'm a comedian...
And I'm an atheist, so I'd be able to look at the
character objectively...

The funny thing is, he was very likely right.

The
Cinema

A few fragments of thought:

C. G. Jung:

> *The cinema, like the detective story, makes it possible to experience without danger all the excitement, passion and desirousness which must be suppressed in a humanitarian ordering of society.*

Orson Welles:

> *It has no boundary...it is a ribbon of dream.*

Dore Schary:

> *The most collaborative of the arts.*

Jean-Luc Godard:

> *Truth twenty-four times a second.*

V. I. Lenin:

> *Of all the arts, the cinema is the most important for us.*

Jean Cocteau:

> *That temple of sex, with its goddesses, its guardians and its victims...*

Sheila Black:

> *An uncomfortable way of watching television.*

Howard Collins (manager in 1953 of Roxy Theatre, N.Y.):

*The film is not an art but a super tabloid for young
and old, moron and genius. Her sister muses are the
comic strips, the pulp magazines, the radio and all
other forms of entertainment based on democratic
rather than aesthetic principles.*

1931

Cinemascope

The wide, wide screen may have saved the industry in 1952, but it came close to killing the art. Hear these justified cries of woe.

Rouben Mamoulian:

> *The worst shape ever devised.*

George Stevens:

> *It's fine if you want a system that shows a boa constrictor to better advantage than a man.*

Samuel Goldwyn:

> *A wide screen makes a bad film twice as bad.*

Fritz Lang:

> *It is a formula for a funeral, or for snakes, but not for human beings.*

Leon Shamroy:

> *It wrecked the art of film for a decade.*

Irving Brecher:

> *Why not keep the screen the same size and reduce the size of the audience?*

Fritz Lang:

> *There was a time when all I looked for was a good story, but nowadays everything has to look the size of Mount Rushmore, and the actors in close-up look as though they belong there.*

Cliches

Quiz

The following lines have come to seem more risible than was the author's original intention. Can you say in what films they originated, and who spoke them?

1 The calla lilies are in bloom again...
2 Nothing like this has come to Rome since Romulus and Remus!
3 When you say that, smile!
4 It seemed like a good idea at the time.
5 Cast adrift in an open boat...
6 I don't need that spear. It's only a young lion.
7 We have ways of making men talk.
8 You're going out a youngster – but you've got to come back a star!
9 You ain't heard nothing yet!
10 These are modern times...1804...
11 Yes, I killed him. And I'm glad, I tell you. Glad, glad, glad!
12 Excuse me while I slip into something more comfortable...
13 If you want anything, just whistle...
14 Café Mozart, eight o'clock.

Answers

1 For years this was included in impersonations of Katharine Hepburn. In fact she did not even speak it in her own character, but in the play within the play in *Stage Door* (1937).

2 A curious lapse on the part of writer-director Joseph L. Mankiewicz, this immortal line was spoken by one member of the crowd to another at the entry into Rome of *Cleopatra* (1962).

3 The ultimate riposte in the nose-to-nose confrontation between Gary Cooper and Walter Huston in *The Virginian* (1930).

4 The earliest use of this I know – and a very effective one – is in a 1931 movie called *The Last Flight*, about a group of American servicemen who hang around Europe after World War I, for want of anything better to do. Slightly shell-shocked, they mostly come to tragic ends, and one of them is gored to death after leaping into the arena during a bullfight. When the journalists outside the hospital ask his friend why the man should have done such a thing, the friend (Richard Barthelmess) says thoughtfully: 'Because it seemed like a good idea at the time.' In this context, the phrase is almost a comment on the futility of war.

5 Who but Charles Laughton as Captain Bligh in the 1935 version of *Mutiny on the Bounty?*

6 Victor Mature in *Samson and Delilah* (1949).

7 Again the earliest use I have come across – and I stand to be corrected – is by Douglass Dumbrille as the evil Mohammed Khan in *Lives of a Bengal Lancer* (1935).

8 Warner Baxter (producer) to Ruby Keeler (chorus girl) as she takes the stage for the ailing star in *42nd Street* (1933).

9 Al Jolson, of course. They are in fact the first words ever spoken on the screen, in the second reel of *The Jazz Singer* (1927).

10 Many costume pictures use this gag, which is usually followed by a joke about income tax having risen to fourpence in the pound. I am unable to date it earlier than *Forever and a Day* (1943) in which it is spoken by Ray Milland.

11 Bette Davis at her most melodramatic, in *The Letter* (1941). They even used the line as catch-phrase on the posters.
12 Jean Harlow to Ben Lyon in *Hell's Angels* (1930).
13 Lauren Bacall to Humphrey Bogart in *To Have and Have Not* (1944).
14 This was the time and place of Harry Lime's fatal appointment in *The Third Man* (1949), though the line is not spoken in the film. It was later used as a joke, notably in *Carry on Spying.*

RENO
STRAIGHT AHEAD

What a Cast!

Lilyan Tashman
Charles 'Buddy'' Rogers
Peggy Shannon
William Boyd
Irving Pichel
Skeets Gallagher
Judith Wood
Wynne Gibson

—and what a story they unfold, a story of marital loves and hates, of drama and comedy, in

A Paramount Picture

'THE ROAD TO RENO''

1931

Harry
Cohn (1891-1958)

When the big boss of Columbia Studios died in 1958, you could take your pick of brickbats and bouquets. The most famous tasteless comment came from Red Skelton on hearing of the huge crowds at Cohn's funeral:

> *It proves what they always say: give the public what they want to see, and they'll come out for it.*

Then there was Hedda Hopper:

> *You had to stand in line to hate him.*

And George Jessel:

> *He was a great showman, and he was a son of a bitch.*

And Elia Kazan:

> *He liked to be the biggest bug in the manure pile.*

And Samuel Goldwyn:

> *He never learned how to live.*

And Budd Schulberg:

> *He was the meanest man I ever knew – an unreconstructed dinosaur.*

But Cohn had a few defenders. There was Artie Shaw:

> *He was a loveable old pirate.*

And, surprisingly, Ethel Barrymore:

He knew the score.

One thing was sure, Cohn thoroughly enjoyed his long tyranny. He said once:

Gower Street is paved with the bones of my executive producers.

And again:

I don't have ulcers: I give them.

Despite his frequent ill-treatment of actors and other creative people, he always averred:

I kiss the feet of talent.

He certainly knew what he wanted, and he had a long record of success. One of his mottoes was:

Let Rembrandt make character studies, not Columbia.

He once said to Daniel Taradash:

Promise me you'll never make a picture where the characters walk out of the room backward.

He claimed:

All I need to make pictures is an office.

In a more self-knowing mood, he admitted:

If I wasn't head of a studio, who would talk to me?

But he concluded:

It's better than being a pimp.

Comedy

Quiz

Film buffs should have no difficulty in tracking down the classic comedies from which these memorable moments emanate...

1 You shouldn't eat chocolates in your condition, Mr ....
It's very bad for you.
  – I had an aunt who ate a box of chocolates every day of her life. She lived to be a hundred and two, and when she had been dead three days, she looked healthier than you do now.
2 If I find a forgotten man first, I win. Is that clear?
3 If we bring a little joy into your humdrum lives, it makes us feel our work ain't been in vain for nothin'.
4 This is the screwiest picture I was ever in.
5 I understand we understand each other.
  – Quite.
6 No beds. They can't have beds!
7 If we had known, we would have greeted you with flowers.
  – Don't make an issue of my womanhood.
8 Behold the walls of Jericho! Maybe not as thick as the ones Joshua blew down with his trumpet, but a lot safer. You see, I have no trumpet.
9 Why, was I so unattractive, so distant, so forbidding?
  – You were extremely attractive, and as for distant and forbidding, quite the reverse, but you were also a little the worse, or better, for wine, and there are rules about that.
10 Remember, men, we're fighting for this woman's honour ...which is probably more than she ever did!

Answers

1 Monty Woolley as the unbearable Sheridan Whiteside in *The Man who came to Dinner* (1941), retorting to Mary Wickes as Miss Treen, the nurse.

2 Gail Patrick as Cornelia in *My Man Godfrey* (1936), a comedy of the depression years in which the idle rich went on a 'scavenger hunt' with human derelicts as trophies. Naturally, the one she finds is only in disguise.

3 Jean Hagen as the intolerable silent movie queen in *Singin' in the Rain* (1952), risking her reputation by opening her mouth at a premiere.

4 Spoken by a camel, straight to camera, in *Road to Morocco* (1942).

5 Understatement can go no further. Henry Daniell and Cary Grant in *The Philadelphia Story* (1940).

6 The redoubtable, diminutive Eva Moore, annoyed at the incursion of strangers into *The Old Dark House* (1932). (Yes, a comedy it really is.)

7 Greta Garbo as the lady comrade in *Ninotchka* (1939), responding to the gallantry of Alexander Granach.

8 Clark Gable in *It Happened One Night* (1934). Claudette Colbert has been forced to spend a night with him in a motel room, but he hangs a blanket on a line between the beds. In the end, of course, the walls come down.

9 *The Philadelphia Story* (1940) again. Katharine Hepburn thinks she misbehaved with James Stewart, but he tells her she simply got a little drunk and he put her to bed. Then she gets mad...

10 Who but Groucho Marx? And to whom would he be referring but Margaret Dumont? The movie is *Duck Soup* (1933).

Gary
Cooper (1901-61)

He was a poet of the real

said Clifford Odets. Whatever that means, it would have embarrassed Cooper. Perhaps Carl Sandburg put it another way:

> *One of the most beloved illiterates this country has ever known.*

Cooper had no very high estimate of his own talent:

> *People ask me how come you been around so long. Well, it's through playing the part of Mr Average Joe American.*

He had Mr Average Joe's reputed insularity:

> *From what I hear about communism, I don't like it because it isn't on the level.*

He distrusted the socialism of plays like *Death of a Salesman*:

> *Sure there are fellows like Willy Loman, but you don't have to write plays about them.*

He enjoyed his niche:

> *Until I came along, all the leading men were handsome, but luckily they wrote a lot of stories about the fellow next door.*

For a man without acting training, he managed very well. King Vidor thought that:

He got a reputation as a great actor just by thinking hard about the next line.

Coop's own explanation was simpler:

To get folks to like you, I figured you sort of had to be their ideal. I don't mean a handsome knight riding a white horse, but a fellow who answered the description of a right guy.

Richard Arlen summed up:

Coop just likes people, it's as simple as that.

Couples

Quiz

Who played the following couples, and in what films?

1 Norman Maine and Vicki Lester in 1937?
2 C. K. Dexter Haven and Tracy Lord in 1940?
3 Charles and Ruth Condomine in 1945?
4 Dr Frederick Steele and Judith Traherne in 1939?
5 Don Birnam and Helen St James in 1945?
6 Joseph and Maria Tura in 1942?
7 Al and Milly Stephenson in 1946?
8 'J.B.' and Dr Constance Peterson in 1945?
9 Immanuel Rath and Lola Frohlich in 1930?
10 Rudolf Rassendyll and Princess Flavia in 1937?
11 Mr and Mrs Maximilian de Winter in 1940?
12 The Ringo Kid and Dallas in 1939?
13 The Duc de Praslin and Henriette Deluzy-Desportes in 1940?
14 Dr Alec Harvey and Laura Jesson in 1946?
15 Yancey and Sabra Cravat in 1930?
16 Walter Neff and Phyllis Dietrichson in 1944?
17 Henry Van Cleve and Martha Strabel in 1943?
18 George Gibbs and Emily Webb in 1940?
19 Major Rama Safti and Lady Edwina Esketh in 1939?
20 Peter Warne and Ellie Andrews in 1934?

Answers

1 Fredric March and Janet Gaynor in *A Star is Born.*
2 Cary Grant and Katharine Hepburn in the *The Philadelphia Story.*
3 Rex Harrison and Constance Cummings in *Blithe Spirit.*
4 George Brent and Bette Davis in *Dark Victory.*
5 Ray Milland and Jane Wyman in *The Lost Weekend.*
6 Jack Benny and Carole Lombard in *To be or Not to Be.*
7 Fredric March and Myrna Loy in *The Best Years of our Lives.*
8 Gregory Peck and Ingrid Bergman in *Spellbound.*
9 Emil Jannings and Marlene Dietrich in *The Blue Angel.*
10 Ronald Colman and Madeleine Carroll in *The Prisoner of Zenda.*
11 Laurence Olivier and Joan Fontaine in *Rebecca.*
12 John Wayne and Claire Trevor in *Stagecoach.*
13 Charles Boyer and Bette Davis in *All This and Heaven Too.*
14 Trevor Howard and Celia Johnson in *Brief Encounter.*
15 Richard Dix and Irene Dunne in *Cimarron.*
16 Fred MacMurray and Barbara Stanwyck in *Double Indemnity.*
17 Don Ameche and Gene Tierney in *Heaven Can Wait.*
18 William Holden and Martha Scott in *Our Town.*
19 Tyrone Power and Myrna Loy in *The Rains Came.*
20 Clark Gable and Claudette Colbert in *It Happened One Night.*

Credits

Quiz

What films had among their credits the following somewhat unusual lines?

1 By William Shakespeare. Additional dialogue by Sam Taylor.
2 Based on an idea by William Shakespeare.
3 After a play by William Shakespeare. Long, long after.
4 This picture is dedicated to the fifty.
5 To the memory of Irving Grant Thalberg we dedicate this, his last great achievement.
6 Co-starring the city of Paris...
7 A film by Otto Preminger [first time].
8 With Mr Joseph Young as himself.
9 Fangs by Dr Ludwig von Krankheit.
10 Introducing James Best.
11 A serio-comic phantasy.
12 A bedpanorama of hospital life.
13 Introducing Alistair Cooke, distinguished journalist and commentator.
14 Academy Award statuettes are used in this picture by permission of the Academy of Motion Picture Arts and Sciences.

1 The 1929 talkie version of *The Taming of the Shrew*, tailored for Mary Pickford and Douglas Fairbanks.

2 *Carry on Cleo* (1964).

3 *The Boys from Syracuse* (1940), derived from *A Comedy of Errors*.

4 *The Great Escape* (1963). In this prisoner-of-war drama, based on fact, the fifty were escaped allied prisoners who were shot by the Gestapo.

5 *The Good Earth* (1938), the film upon which Thalberg was working at the time of his death. This posthumous credit was the only one he ever took.

6 *The Man on the Eiffel Tower*, a curious American thriller made in 1950 and starring Charles Laughton as Inspector Maigret.

7 *The Man with the Golden Arm* (1956). The credit caused a great deal of comment in Hollywood, not least from Nelson Algren, author of the original novel; it was the first time a producer or director had claimed authorship of a movie.

8 *Mighty Joe Young* (1949), the comedy successor to *King Kong*.

9 *The Fearless Vampire Killers* (1967). Fortunately or not, this kind of humour was not carried through into the film.

10 *Three on a Couch*, a 1967 Jerry Lewis comedy. The strange thing was that Mr Best scarcely needed introducing, having been a familiar face in movies and TV for the previous ten years.

11 *Son of Kong* (1933), the hurried sequel to *King Kong*. Compared to its original it was so weak that its makers decided to present it, rather tentatively, as a comedy.

12 *Carry on Doctor* (1968).

13 *The Three Faces of Eve* (1957).

14 *A Star is Born* (1954).

Critics

Very little film criticism is quotable: at its best it is an expression of personality rather than wit. The reviews one remembers tend to be the scathing ones, especially those dismissive one-liners which are really unforgivable but linger over the arch of years:

> I Am a Camera. *Me no Leica.*
> Lost in a Harem. *But with Abbott and Costello.*
> Aimez-vous Brahms? *Brahms, oui.*
> Ben Hur. *Loved Ben, hated Hur.*
> Samson and Delilah. *A movie for de Millions.*
> Bill and Coo. *By conservative estimate, one of the God-damnedest things ever seen.*

The authors of these pearls are now, by me, forgotten, with the exception of the last, which came from the pen of James Agee, a lamented American writer whose economical, literate reviews delighted all film enthusiasts in the forties and established a few Hollywood reputations. His collected reviews should all be read with affection; here we can spare room for four of his more waspish put-downs:

> Random Harvest. *I would like to recommend this film to those who can stay interested in Ronald Colman's amnesia for two hours and who could with pleasure eat a bowl of Yardley's shaving soap for breakfast.*
>
> *During the making of* Pin Up Girl *Betty Grable was in an early stage of pregnancy – and everyone else was evidently in a late stage of paresis.*
>
> Tycoon. *Several tons of dynamite are set off in this picture – none of it under the right people.*

You Were Meant For Me. *That's what you think.*

Two more moments of invective. First, *Variety* on Hedy Lamarr's independent production *The Strange Woman*:

> *Hedy bit off more than she could chew, so the chewing was done by the rest of the cast, and what was chewed was the scenery.*

And Pamela Kellino on *The Egyptian*:

> *One of those great big rotten pictures Hollywood keeps on turning out.*

Now for some self-criticism. Joseph L. Mankiewicz on his own movie *Cleopatra*:

> *This picture was conceived in a state of emergency, shot in confusion, and wound up in blind panic.*

He also called it:

> *The toughest three pictures I ever made.*

Ethel Barrymore, when asked her opinion of *Rasputin and the Empress*, in which she co-starred with her brothers Lionel and John, replied:

> *I thought I was pretty good, but what those two boys were up to I'll never know.*

Erich Von Stroheim reminiscing on his own much-mutilated picture *Greed*:

> *When ten years later I saw the film myself, it was like seeing a corpse in a graveyard.*

Otto Preminger on *Saint Joan*:

> *My most distinguished flop. I've had much less distinguished ones.*

45

And Victor Fleming, director of *Gone with the Wind*, refusing David O. Selznick's offer of a percentage of the profits instead of salary:

> *Don't be a damn fool, David. This picture is going to be one of the biggest white elephants of all time.*

Similarly misguided was Adolph Zukor when he first read the script of *Broken Blossoms*:

> *You bring me a picture like this and want money for it? You may as well put your hand in my pocket and steal it. It isn't commercial. Everyone in it dies.*

I can recall only three memorable items of praise. Cecilia Ager on *Citizen Kane*:

> *It's as though you had never seen a movie before.*

Terry Ramsaye on *Intolerance*:

> *The only film fugue.*

And Woodrow Wilson on *The Birth of a Nation*:

> *Like writing history with lightning. And it's all true.*

My own favourite critiques also include Sarah Bernhardt's enthusiastic remark when she saw her 1912 version of *Queen Elizabeth*:

> *Mr Zukor, you have put the best of me in pickle for all time.*

And the remark of macabre New Yorker cartoonist Charles Addams, when asked his opinion after the premiere of *Cleopatra*:

> *I only came to see the asp.*

Bette
Davis (1908-   )

For a girl with no looks, Bette Davis rose fast to the top and stayed there a long time. When she first arrived in Hollywood the official greeter missed her at the station, and his later excuse was:

No one faintly like an actress got off the train.

Carl Laemmle is credited with two waspish remarks about her:

I can't imagine any guy giving her a tumble.

And:

She has as much sex appeal as Slim Summerville.

She herself confesses:

When I saw my first film test I ran from the projection room screaming.

She finally settled for a career without glamour:

I was the first star who ever came out of the water looking wet.

Nobody knew what I looked like because I never looked the same way twice.

Determination carried her through. As her later husband Gary Merrill said:

Whatever Bette had chosen to do in life, she would

47

have had to be the top or she couldn't have endured it.

She admitted this herself:

If Hollywood didn't work out I was all prepared to be the best secretary in the world.

As David Zinman summarises:

All she had going for her was her talent.

But by 1937 she was at the top of the tree, dishing out hell to those who had dished it out to her. Said her once co-star Brian Aherne:

Surely no one but a mother could have loved Bette Davis at the height of her career.

Definitions

A selection, chosen for entertainment rather than instruction.

AGENT : *A guy who is sore because an actor gets ninety per cent of what he makes.*

CASTING : *Deciding which of two faces the public is least tired of.*

DOUBLE FEATURE : *A show that enables you to sit through a picture you don't care to see, so you can see one you don't like. — Henry Morgan*

DISNEYLAND : *The biggest people trap ever built by a mouse.*

EPIC : *The easiest kind of picture to make badly. — Charlton Heston*

FANS : *People who tell an actor he's not alone in the way he feels about himself.*

IT : *The indefinable something. — Elinor Glyn, creator of 'It'*

MUSICALS : *A series of catastrophes ending with a floor show. — Oscar Levant*

OOMPH : *The sound a fat man makes when he bends over to tie his laces in a phone booth. — Ann Sheridan*

TELEVISION : *A medium, so called because it is neither rare nor well done. — Ernie Kovacs*

ROMANOFF'S RESTAURANT : *A place where a man can take his wife and family and have a lovely seven-course meal for $3,400. — George Jessel*

49

Cecil B.
De Mille (1881-1959)

Ready when you are, Mr de Mille.

It's the tag line of a long shaggy dog story, the purpose of which is to establish de Mille as the producer of enormous, stagey biblical epics. Towards the end of his life he did submerge himself in this role, but his career embraced almost every kind of movie, notably the sex comedy, in which after World War I he made a small corner. Whatever the show, he made a success of it, and he was respected throughout Hollywood as a disciplinarian who always got his films out under budget. There was a joke during World War II:

Anyone who leaves de Mille for the armed forces is a slacker.

He is credited with sending back a writer's script and attaching a terrifying cover note:

What I have crossed out I didn't like. What I haven't crossed out I am dissatisfied with.

He exercised supreme control over his stars, and once said to Paulette Goddard:

Remember you are a star. Never go across the alley even to dump garbage unless you are dressed to the teeth.

He told his staff:

You are here to please me. Nothing else on earth matters.

50

He went to extreme lengths to prove his authority. Arthur Miller thought:

> *I never met such an egotist in my life. Even if he was wrong and knew it, once he said it it had to be.*

His brother William was awed by his ambition and achievement:

> *The trouble with Cecil is that he always bites off more than he can chew – and then chews it.*

The same William cast a wry eye on Cecil's first bible picture in the twenties:

> *Having attended to the underclothes, bathrooms and matrimonial irregularities of his fellow citizens, he now began to consider their salvation.*

Even when Cecil dealt with heavenly themes, he kept his feet on earth. He said to a scriptwriter:

> *It's just a damn good hot tale, so don't get a lot of thees, thous and thums on your mind.*

His comparative ignorance of his favourite subject provoked a much-repeated clerihew:

> *Cecil B. de Mille*
> *Much against his will*
> *Was persuaded to keep Moses*
> *Out of the Wars of the Roses.*

He saw the Bible as a ready-made script factory:

> *Give me any couple of pages of the Bible and I'll give you a picture.*

He took neither credit nor blame for his themes:

> *I didn't write the Bible and didn't invent sin.*

He was also quite clear where his support lay:

I make my pictures for people, not for critics.

His approach to actresses was on similarly direct lines. In 1934, when he thought of Claudette Colbert as Cleopatra, he said to her:

How would you like to be the wickedest woman in history?

But he knew that what really mattered to a movie is not the star but the producer:

A picture is made a success not on a set but over the drawing board.

1932

Dialogue

From internal evidence, elephantine memory, or plain guess-
work, please name the actors who spoke the following lines,
and also name the films.

1 Most girls would give their eyes to see Monte.
     –Wouldn't that rather defeat the purpose?
2 I've never been so insulted in all my life.
     –Well, it's early yet.
3 You're the most beautiful plank in your husband's plat-
     form.
     –That's a heck of a thing to call a woman!
4 I have a confession to make to you. Baron, you are a crook.
     You robbed the gentleman in room 253, 5, 7 and 9.
     –Countess, believe me, before you left this room I would
     have told you everything. And let me say this with love in
     my heart – Countess, you are a thief...
5 You don't understand...every night when the moon is full,
     I turn into a wolf.
     –You and fifty million other guys!
6 You used to be in pictures. You used to be big.
     –I am big. It's the pictures that got small.
7 Do you know I read somewhere that machinery is going to
     take the place of every profession?
     –Oh, my dear, that's something *you'll never* have to worry
     about.
8 You don't love me any more, do you?
     – That is an ungallant question which women always want
     answered gallantly.
9 How's you little flowers making out?
     –We's okay, Lawd.
10 In these days, old man, nobody thinks in terms of human
     beings. Governments don't, so why should we? They talk of

the people and the proletariat, and I talk of the mugs. It's the same thing. They have their five year plans and so have I.

–You used to believe in a God.

–Oh, I still *believe*, old man. In God and Mercy and all that. The Dead are happier dead. They don't miss much here, poor devils.

11 Pity he had no children.

–Oh, but I have. Thousands of them. And all boys.

12 ...Shows what I say is true. No difference between the sexes. None. Men, women. The same.

– They are, huh?

Well, maybe there *is* a difference. But it's a little difference.

– Yuh. Well, as the French say.

How do they say?

– *Vive la différence!*

Which means?

– Which means: hurray for that little difference!

13 Oh, I wish I were a woman of thirty-six, dressed in black satin, with a string of pearls.

– You would not be here with me if you were.

14 Boss, you're in danger. Your life is hanging on a thread.

– So are my pants.

You're gonna get killed.

– I wish they'd tell me these things. I don't mind being killed, but I resent hearing it from a character whose head comes to a point.

15 I really can't go on accepting these gifts, though you're awfully kind.

– I'm not kind. I never give anything without expecting something in return. I always get paid.

16 Must you flirt?

– I don't have to, but I find it natural.

Suppress it.

– I'll try.

For my own information would you call your approach towards me typical of the local morale?

– Madame, it is that kind of approach which has made Paris what it is.

Answers

1 A silly remark and a smooth answer: Florence Bates and Laurence Olivier in *Rebecca* (1940).

2 Groucho Marx gets in everywhere. The insulted lady is Esther Muir, and the film is *A Day at the Races* (1937).

3 A political comedy, *State of the Union* (1948). The speakers are Adolphe Menjou and Katharine Hepburn.

4 This has the delightful smell of high comedy from a gentler era. It has in fact the Lubitsch touch, being from *Trouble in Paradise* (1932), written by Samson Raphaelson. The speakers are Miriam Hopkins and Herbert Marshall.

5 When did Lon Chaney as the wolfman meet with wisecracks? In *Abbott and Costello meet Frankenstein* (1948), when he tried out his familiar routine on Lou Costello.

6 William Holden and Gloria Swanson in *Sunset Boulevard* (1950).

7 The famous conclusion to *Dinner at Eight* (1933). Good timer Jean Harlow exchanges small talk with Marie Dressler, and gets more than she bargained for.

8 It has to be Noel Coward, and it is, in *The Scoundrel* (1935); the lady is Julie Haydon.

9 Rex Ingram as De Lawd inspecting his universe in *Green Pastures* (1936).

10 The clue here is the phrase 'old man'. In fact this is the summit of Orson Welles' argument to Joseph Cotten in the Ferris wheel sequence of *The Third Man* (1949).

11 *Goodbye Mr Chips* (1939), with Robert Donat rallying briefly from his deathbed.

12 Katharine Hepburn and Spencer Tracy in *Adam's Rib* (1949).

13 *Rebecca* again: Joan Fontaine and Laurence Olivier.

14 Easy: Chico and Groucho Marx in *A Night in Casablanca* (1945).

15 Vivien Leigh and Clark Gable in *Gone With the Wind* (1939).

16 Greta Garbo and Melvyn Douglas in *Ninotchka* (1939).

Directors

A selection of directorial attitudes:

> *I'm interested in people, the way they behave. Other directors get their effects by showing doorknobs being turned, things like that. I like to concentrate on the actors' faces. — George Cukor*

> *I feel very strongly that the director is supposed to be the boss. Art was never created by democracy. — Charlton Heston*

> *Don't get excited. Obstacles make a better picture. — Victor Fleming*

> *You can have all the philosophy you like: if a film doesn't come across in graphic terms, it falls short. — Rouben Mamoulian*

> *He never once looked in the camera when we worked together. You see the man had bad eyes, as long as I knew him, but he was a man whose veins ran with the business. — Arthur Miller (photographer) on John Ford*

> *There is no suspense like the suspense of a delayed coition. — D. W. Griffith*

> *I don't try to guess what a million people will like. It's hard enough to know what I like. — John Huston*

> *Always cast against the part and it won't be boring. — David Lean*

Film-making has become a kind of hysterical pregnancy. – Richard Lester

I am never quite sure whether I am one of the cinema's elder statesmen or just the oldest whore on the beat. – Joseph L. Mankiewicz

The best films are best because of nobody but the director. – Roman Polanski

"MOROCCO"
WITH
GARY COOPER
MARLENE DIETRICH
ADOLPHE MENJOU

A Paramount Picture

Every man's past is his own secret in the Foreign Legion — but this w o m a n makes the past live.

1930

Epitaphs

Over the years, a few stars have been nudged by the press into composing their own epitaphs. Herewith a selection of this grave humour.

*He was an average guy who could carry a tune. –
Bing Crosby*

*On the whole, I'd rather be in Philadelphia. – W. C.
Fields*

He was lucky – and he knew it. – Cary Grant

*A nice part – only four 'sides', but good company
and in for a long run. – Edward Everett Horton*

*Well, I've played everything but a harp. – Lionel
Barrymore*

This is too deep for me. – Hedy Lamarr

Excuse my dust. – Dorothy Parker

Did you hear about my operation? – Warner Baxter

*Here's something I want to get off my chest. –
William Haines*

*A gentleman farmer goes back to the soil. – Lewis
Stone*

Do not disturb. – Constance Bennett

At last I get top billing. – Wallace Ford

Now I've laid me down to die
I pray my neighbours not to pry
Too deeply into sins that I
Not only cannot here deny
But much enjoyed as time flew by...
— Preston Sturges

1933

Fade-Outs

Quiz
The last line of a movie is likely to be the most memorable. Can you name the actors who spoke the following lines, and say what movies they ended?

1 I guess Rosebud is just a piece in a jigsaw puzzle...a missing piece.
2 Hello. Clara?
3 O'Lan, you are the earth.
4 Every word that boy said is the truth. I'm not fit for office!
5 Look, Ma – top of the world!
6 The lobsters are back!
7 I steal...
8 Madness! Madness!
9 This is Mrs Norman Maine...
10 It was beauty killed the beast.
11 All right, Mr de Mille, I'm ready for my close up now.
12 Now for Australia and a crack at those Japs!
13 After all, tomorrow is another day...
14 Darling, you're crying. I believe you're really sentimental after all.
15 This is the people's war! It is our war! We are the fighters! Fight it, then! Fight it with all that is in us! And God defend the right!
16 You can't hurt me. I always wear a bullet-proof vest around the studio.
17 She was beautiful when she died...a hundred years ago.
18 Can't lick us. Can't wipe us out. We'll go on forever. 'Cause we're the people.
19 Always the same. People come, people go. Nothing ever happens.
20 That's the dumbest thing I ever heard...

1 No prizes for naming the film: Rosebud points only to *Citizen Kane* (1941). But the speaker? The reporter, Thompson, played by William Alland who later became a producer at Universal.

2 Obviously a phone call...the one made by Ernest Borgnine at the end of *Marty* (1955) when he has decided that he means to continue his friendship with the plain girl played by Betsy Blair.

3 Paul Muni's final speech to the stars in *The Good Earth* (1937). His wife O'Lan, played by Luise Rainer, has just died.

4 Difficult because, although these are the last clear lines of dialogue in the movie, they are followed by two or three minutes of shouting and general hubbub. The speaker is Claude Rains, playing corrupt Senator Paine in *Mr Smith goes to Washington* (1939). His admission, in full Senate, brings wild rejoicing from all concerned, and the film ends with a shot of Harry Carey, as president of the assembly, giving up his attempt to restore order and relaxing in his chair with a smile. The published script has subsequent wind-up scenes, but they were either deleted before the premiere or never filmed.

5 James Cagney as the psychopathic mother-fixated gangster Cody Jarrett in *White Heat* (1949), as he blows himself up by firing a bullet into the giant gas cylinder on top of which he has been cornered by police.

6 Practically impossible, but irresistible. It comes from a 1956 Rank British film *High Tide at Noon*, set in the lobster fishing communities of Nova Scotia. The young lovers are separated by various complications including the disappearance of lobsters from the locality. The heroine returns years later, to be greeted with this ecstatic news by her boy friend Michael Craig, and the scene fades out on a seaside clinch and track-back which should figure in any collector's compendium of cliches.

7 Paul Muni in *I am a Fugitive From a Chain Gang* (1932). At the end of the film, a victim of circumstance, he has been on the run for years, when one night he meets again his old girl friend. 'What do you do now?' she asks help-

lessly. 'I steal...' is his chilling reply as he fades into the darkness.

8 Jack Hawkins at the end of *The Bridge on the River Kwai* (1958), by which time the intentions of the leading characters are vague enough to give his remark a double meaning.

9 Either Janet Gaynor or Judy Garland; in other words, one of the versions of *A Star is Born* (1937 or 1954). As a starlet, the heroine has married top Hollywood actor Norman Maine, whose star has declined as rapidly as hers has risen. He finally commits suicide; and at the subsequent Oscar ceremony she accepts her award under his name.

10 Robert Armstrong as Carl Denham speaking the epitaph on *King Kong* (1933) as the monster ape lies dead at the foot of the Empire State Building.

11 Gloria Swanson as Norma Desmond in *Sunset Boulevard* (1950). The ageing film star has killed her lover and become quite mad, so that as she descends the stairs to the waiting police cars she imagines that the newspaper photographers are studio cameramen waiting to capture her beauty.

12 This has to be Errol Flynn, and it is. The film is *Desperate Journey* (1942), the scene an aeroplane as he speeds back to England after apparently decimating the Nazi strength in Germany.

13 Vivien Leigh as Scarlett O'Hara in *Gone with the Wind* (1939). Of course.

14 Heather Sears in *Room at the Top* (1959). Her bridegroom Joe Lampton has made her pregnant and got what he always wanted, money and prestige; but as they drive away in the wedding car and she sees a tear in his eye, she does not realize that he is thinking of his dead mistress, the only woman he has really loved.

15 I doubt whether anyone would guess the source of this quote as *Mrs Miniver* (1942). The film ends on a service in the bombed village church, and these are the last words of the sermon preached by Henry Wilcoxon.

16 Yes, *Hellzapoppin* (1942). Elisha Cook has just been pumped full of bullets when he makes this calm remark. He then drinks a glass of water, which spurts out from a score of holes as the film fades out.

17 Edward Van Sloan as he stands by the body of *Dracula's Daughter* (1936) and agrees with Otto Kruger's comment about her beauty.

18 One of the most famous fadeout speeches in films: Jane Darwell as the indomitable Ma Joad in *Grapes of Wrath* (1940).

19 Irony, of course. A great deal did happen to the people in *Grand Hotel* (1933), but doorman Jean Hersholt didn't know about it.

20 *What's Up, Doc?* (1972). This is Ryan O'Neal's reaction to the use by Barbra Streisand of his own famous line from *Love Story*, 'Love means never having to say you're sorry'.

Douglas
Fairbanks (1883-1939)

Quotes about the elder Fairbanks all point the same way: despite his comparatively short stature, he was much larger than life.

He has such verve. We can use his body.

said D. W. Griffith. From that day Fairbanks kept himself in rigorous training, believing that:

The man that's out to do something has to keep in high gear all the time.

He managed. An anonymous critic in 1920 put his finger on the Fairbanks magic:

He smiles, and you feel relieved.

Alistair Cooke called him:

A sort of Ariel.

and added:

At a difficult period in American history, Douglas Fairbanks appeared to know all the answers.

Famous
Roles

Say who, in what films:

1 Played Regina Giddens, Catherine the Great...and said 'Fasten your seat belts, it's going to be a bumpy night.'
2 Played Alfred Kralik, Elwood P. Dowd...and said 'The prettiest sight in this fine pretty world is the sight of the privileged class enjoying its privileges.'
3 Played Sam Spade, Roy Earle...and said 'A press agent is many things, most of them punishable by law.'
4 Played Catherine Earnshaw, Lady Blakeney...and said 'Frederic, you must stop this Polonaise jangle!'
5 Played Louis Renault, Job Skeffington...and said 'Any more objections to the new tax, from our Saxon friends?'
6 Played Martin Snyder, Rocky Sullivan...and said 'My mother thanks you, my father thanks you, my sister thanks you and I thank you.'
7 Played Tony Camonte, Professor Joseph Elsner...and said 'Not only is an innocent man crying out for justice; but more, much more – a great nation is in desperate danger of forfeiting her honour!'
8 Played Dona St Columb, Tessa Sanger...and said 'You didn't love her! You didn't love her!'
9 Played Mike Conovan, Major Robert Rogers...and said 'They're murderers. I know the law says they're not because I'm still alive, but that's not their fault.'
10 Played Sam Grunion, Gordon Miller...and said 'Oh, no, not for me, three men on a horse.'
11 Played Dan Roman, Sergeant John M. Stryker...and said 'I watched you with that baby – that other woman's baby. You looked – well, nice.'
12 Played James Corbett, Captain Geoffrey Vickers...and said 'It's injustice I hate, not Normandy.'

Answers

1 Bette Davis: *The Little Foxes, John Paul Jones, All About Eve*

2 James Stewart: *The Shop around the Corner, Harvey, The Philadelphia Story*

3 Humphrey Bogart: *The Maltese Falcon, High Sierra, The Barefoot Contessa*

4 Merle Oberon: *Wuthering Heights, The Scarlet Pimpernel, A Song to Remember*

5 Claude Rains: *Casablanca, Mr Skeffington, The Adventures of Robin Hood*

6 James Cagney: *Love Me or Leave Me, Angels with Dirty Faces, Yankee Doodle Dandy*

7 Paul Muni: *Scarface, A Song to Remember, The Life of Emile Zola*

8 Joan Fontaine: *Frenchman's Creek, The Constant Nymph, Rebecca*

9 Spencer Tracy: *Pat and Mike, Northwest Passage, Fury*

10 Groucho Marx: *Love Happy, Room Service, A Day at the Races*

11 John Wayne: *The High and the Mighty, Sands of Iwo Jima, Stagecoach*

12 Errol Flynn: *Gentleman Jim, The Charge of the Light Brigade, The Adventures of Robin Hood*

W. C. Fields (1879-1946)

Today the centre of a cult which would have astonished him,
W. C. Fields was one of life's genuine oddballs, able to see the
funny side of his own misanthropy and to turn it to commercial
use. In most of his films he was straitjacketed, but the few he
controlled personally are uniquely Fieldsian, anarchic and
paceless, fantasticated versions of his unyielding private life with
a few in-jokes for good measure. They feature such characters
as

J. Frothingham Waterbury
Ogg Ogilvie
Filthy McNasty
Ouliotta Haemoglobin
F. Snoopington Pinkerton
Elmer Prettywillie
T. Frothingell Bellows
A. Pismo Clam
Ambrose Wolfinger
Egbert Souse
Cuthbert J. Twillie
Larson E. Whipsnade

Fields' own pseudonyms, either for professional use on his
screenplays or merely to conceal a new bank account, include

Primrose Magoo
Mahatma Kane Jeeves
Otis Criblecoblis
Ampico J. Steinway
Charles Bogle
Felton J. Satchelstern

He had a splendid command of the English language which

effectively silenced criticisms when he was cast as Micawber in *David Copperfield*. His nasal delivery and orotund phrasing were imitated the world over, and they are essential to the effectiveness of such oft-quoted lines as:

> *I must have a drink of breakfast.*

or:

> *Somebody left the cork out of my lunch.*

or (of an elderly lady dressed to kill):

> *She's all done up like a well kept grave.*

or:

> *I exercise extreme self control. I never drink anything stronger than gin before breakfast.*

or:

> *If at first you don't succeed, try again. Then quit. No use being a damn fool about it.*

or:

> *There's an Ethiopian in the fuel supply.*

or:

> *I never vote for anyone. I always vote against.*

His oaths were splendid, consisting of such watered-down versions of profanity as 'Godfrey Daniel!' or 'Great Mother of Pearl!' He was indeed a profane and outlandish man. When his lady neighbour in Beverly Hills came out to remonstrate with him for standing in the middle of his new green lawn and shooting the singing birds with a rifle, he is alleged to have growled:

*I'll go on shooting the bastards till they learn to shit
green...*

When another lady, an inquiring journalist this time, asked
why he never drank water, he gave the simple reason:

Fish f— in it

He occasionally mentioned to acquaintances that he was involved in charity work, and when asked what charity he would
murmur: 'The F.E.B.F.' When an explanation of the initials
was requested, it was given as:

F— Everyone but Fields.

As his biographer Robert Lewis Taylor said:

*His main purpose seemed to be to break as many
rules as possible and cause the maximum amount of
trouble for everybody.*

He hated children and animals, and once said of a churlish
friend:

*Anyone who hates small dogs and children can't be
all bad.*

It is of course alleged that when co-starring with Baby Le Roy
he spiked the infant's milk with gin, and when Le Roy proved
unfit for further work that day stalked around yelling:

The kid's no trouper!

Film of
the Book

Quiz

Many films are retitled and rewritten from less famous books. Can you name the films made from the following?

1 *The Wheel Spins* by Ethel Lina White
2 *The Midwich Cuckoos* by John Wyndham
3 *The Gun* by C. S. Forester
4 *Killing a Mouse on Sunday* by Emeric Pressburger
5 *The Brick Foxhole* by Richard Brooks
6 *Benighted* by J. B. Priestley
7 *The Curse of Capistrano* by Johnston McCulley
8 *Mute Witness* by Robert L. Pike
9 *Glory for Me* by Mackinlay Kantor
10 *Sobbin' Women* by Stephen Vincent Benet
11 *The Light of Day* by Eric Ambler
12 *Stage to Lordsburg* by Ernest Haycox
13 *A Mule for the Marquesa* by Frank O'Rourke
14 *Seven and a Half Cents* by Richard Bissell
15 *Night Bus* by Samuel Hopkins Adams
16 *The Small Woman* by Alan Burgess
17 *Washington Square* by Henry James
18 *Personal History* by Vincent Sheean
19 *The Secret Agent* by Joseph Conrad
20 *Red Alert* by Peter George
21 *The House of Dr Edwardes* by Francis Beeding
22 *Hell's Playground* by Vera Simonton
23 *A Shilling for Candles* by Josephine Tey
24 *Man Running* by Selwyn Jepson
25 *Bad Time at Hondo* by Don Maguire
26 *The Basement Room* by Graham Greene

Answers

1 Hitchcock's *The Lady Vanishes* (1938)
2 *Village of the Damned*
3 *The Pride and the Passion*
4 *Behold a Pale Horse*
5 *Crossfire*
6 *The Old Dark House*
7 *The Mark of Zorro*
8 *Bullitt*
9 *The Best Years of our Lives*
10 *Seven Brides for Seven Brothers*
11 *Topkapi*
12 *Stagecoach*
13 *The Professionals*
14 *The Pajama Game*
15 *It Happened One Night*
16 *The Inn of the Sixth Happiness*
17 *The Heiress*
18 *Foreign Correspondent*
19 *Sabotage* (U.S. title *A Woman Alone*). When he made this film in 1937, Hitchcock was unable to use the original title, as only the previous year he had made a quite different film called *Secret Agent*.
20 *Dr Strangelove*
21 Hitchcock's *Spellbound*
22 *White Cargo*
23 Hitchcock's *Young and Innocent* (*The Girl Was Young*)
24 Hitchcock's *Stage Fright*
25 *Bad Day at Black Rock*
26 *The Fallen Idol*

First
Lines

Quiz

What films began with the following narration? The first group are spoken by an unseen storyteller.

1 Deep among the lonely sunbaked hills of Texas the great and weatherbeaten stone still stands...
2 I never knew the old Vienna before the war, with its Strauss music, its glamour and easy charm...Constantinople suited me better.
3 Come closer! [There's a catch here! –Ed.]
4 Call me Ishmael...
5 Last night I dreamed I went to Manderley again...
6 Our story takes us down this shadowed path to a dark and guarded building in the British midlands...

The following are put up on the screen to be read:

7 This is a Halloween tale of Brooklyn, where anything can happen, and usually does...
8 This picture is dedicated to all the beautiful women in the world who have shot their husbands full of holes out of pique...
9 The first law of every being is to preserve itself and live. You sow hemlock, and you live to see ears of corn ripen. – *Machiavelli*
10 New York, skyscraper champion of the world, where the slickers and know-it-alls peddle gold bricks to each other and truth, crushed to earth, rises more phoney than a glass eye...
11 This story takes place in Paris, in those wonderful days when a siren was a brunette and not an alarm...and when a Frenchman turned out the lights, it wasn't because of an air raid...

72

12 This is a story of the period between two world wars – an interim during which insanity cut loose, liberty took a nose dive, and humanity was kicked around somewhat...

13 This concerns the destruction of an empire, brought about by the mad ambition of one man. A few of the characters are still alive. The rest met death by violence.

14 In the seventeenth century Holland was a world power, her ships carried treasure to Amsterdam from all over the world, but her proudest glory was the son of a miller from Leyden...

15 This is the story of that unconquerable fortress – the American home, 1943.

16 This is a story of passion, bloodshed, desire and death – everything, in fact that makes life worth living.

17 To the Commandos and Airborne Troops of Great Britain – the spirit of whose actions it has been humbly attempted to recapture in some ensuing scenes – this film is dedicated.

1 *Duel in the Sun*. Narrator, Orson Welles.
2 *The Third Man*. Narrator, – no, not Joseph Cotten, but Trevor Howard.
3 Very difficult. Forty-year-old film buffs will remember that Warners used to make trailers for all their thrillers starting with Sidney Greenstreet in a far-off spotlight. 'Come closer,' he said, 'I have a tale to unfold...' Needless to say the trailer was usually better than the film.
4 *Moby Dick*. Narrator, in the 1956 version, Richard Basehart.
5 The most famous first line in film history: *Rebecca*, of course. Narrator, Joan Fontaine.
6 *Random Harvest*. The dark and guarded house is a military mental asylum. Narrator uncredited.
7 *Arsenic and Old Lace*.
8 *Roxie Hart*.
9 *Little Caesar*.
10 *Nothing Sacred*. Ben Hecht's style is inimitable.
11 *Ninotchka*.
12 Another unmistakable style – Chaplin's. The film, *The Great Dictator*.
13 *Rasputin and the Empress*.
14 *Rembrandt*.
15 *Since You Went Away*.
16 *Irma la Douce*.
17 Olivier's *Henry V*.

Errol
Flynn (1909-59)

He was one of the wild characters of the world.

said Ann Sheridan. His wicked wicked ways were well known,
but nobody ever admitted to disliking him for them; perhaps
because, as Jack L. Warner said:

> *To the Walter Mittys of the world he was all the
> heroes in one magnificent, sexy, animal package.*

Old drinking cronies like David Niven (who shared with him a
house called Cirrhosis-by-the-sea) and Peter Finch still talk of
him with affection. Lewis Milestone perhaps exaggerated
slightly when he said:

> *His faults harmed no one but himself.*

But even the people he did jar against seem to have borne
him little ill-will, with the possible exception of the Australian
creditors from whom he escaped before going to Hollywood.
In a later broadcast to the people down under, he said
jovially:

> *If there's anyone listening to whom I owe money,
> I'm prepared to forget it if you are.*

A lot of people certainly looked at him and tut-tutted. Herbert
Wilcox thought that:

> *His love of life defeated his ability as an artist.*

And Leslie Mallory described his life as:

> *A fifty-year trespass against good taste.*

There were other ways of looking at his behaviour. One of his wives, Nora Eddington, said rather proudly:

> *He wasn't afraid of anything, particularly if there was a challenge to it.*

Some of the things he did were a reaction against being under-employed:

> *I felt like an impostor, taking all that money for reciting ten or twelve lines of nonsense a day.*

He defended himself blithely:

> *The public has always expected me to be a playboy, and a decent chap never lets his public down.*

And:

> *Women won't let me stay single, and I won't let myself stay married.*

He exaggerated cheerfully in the cause of publicity:

> *I allow myself to be understood as a colourful fragment in a drab world.*

But he was determined to have a good time:

> *I'll live this half of my life, I don't care about the other half.*

And at the end he could say:

> *I've had a hell of a lot of fun, and I've enjoyed every minute of it.*

At his passing, Tony Britton cabled Trevor Howard:

> *Old Errol died laughing. Can you beat that?*

Funny
Men

Quiz

Comedians are often accused of stealing each other's gags, but in fact a good comic is inseparable from his own material. The following lines are all typical of their proprietors, a formidable array of leading laughtermakers. Which? And in which films?

1 Lemonade...in a dirty glass!
2 I brought you some hard boiled eggs and some nuts.
3 Everybody wants to get into the act!
4 Get your tuttsi-fruttsi ice cream...
5 So they call me Concentration Camp Erhardt?
6 Either this guy's dead or my watch has stopped.
7 I'm a ba-a-a-a-ad boy!
8 Oh, calamity...
9 Who will be the next to outwit me? This is a game of chance...
10 I'm a controversial figure. My friends either dislike me or hate me.

1 Bob Hope in a crowded bar in *Road to Utopia*, trying not to be thought a sissy.
2 Stan Laurel visiting Oliver Hardy in *County Hospital*, obviously about to be no comfort at all.
3 Jimmy Durante in almost every film he made.
4 Chico Marx, Hollywood's only Jewish Italian, in *A Day at the Races*.
5 Jack Benny playing for time in *To Be or not to Be*.
6 Groucho Marx, also in *A Day at the Races*, pretending to be a doctor but unable to resist a crack.
7 Lou Costello's inevitable cry of self-reproach.
8 A line delivered in Robertson Hare's plummiest tones at each impending disaster.
9 W. C. Fields issuing sucker bait in *It's a Gift*.
10 Oscar Levant, self-styled 'the world's oldest child prodigy'. He also said, of his role in *Humoresque*, 'I played an unsympathetic part – myself.'

Clark
Gable (1901-60)

The King of Hollywood? He modestly disclaimed the title, but there was sense to it: he always seemed to be in charge. As the *New York Times* said:

> *Gable was as certain as the sunrise. He was consistently and stubbornly all man.*

He said himself:

> *The only reason they come to see me is that I know life is great – and they know I know it.*

And again:

> *I'm no actor and I never have been. What people see on the screen is me.*

What they saw, they liked. Publicity man Ralph Wainwright said:

> *All of his life people turned around to stare at him.*

This was remarkable considering his famous physical drawback, well phrased by Howard Hughes:

> *His ears made him look like a taxicab with both doors open.*

Milton Berle called him:

> *The best ears of our lives.*

It didn't stop him from influencing the world, and not only the female half of it. Historian Frederick Lewis Allen recalled that:

> *When Clark Gable in* It Happened One Night *disclosed that he wore no undershirt, the knitwear manufacturers rocked from the shock to their sales.*

Gable himself summed up:

> *This King stuff is pure bull. I eat and drink and go to the bathroom just like anybody else. I'm just a lucky slob from Ohio who happened to be in the right place at the right time.*

Ziegfeld, himself, presents you with this gorgeous entertainment. A see and hear delight. American girls glorified before your eyes. An extravaganza-revue-romance. Dances originated by Ted Shawn. Walter Donaldson-Irving Berlin song hits. Eddie Cantor, Helen Morgan, Rudy Vallee in REVUE scenes. Lavish sets in TECHNICOLOR. A New Show World sensation.

1929

Glamour
Girls

Some thoughts on the subject.

Adolph Zukor of Clara Bow:

> *She danced even when her feet were not moving.*

Deanna Durbin, in 1959, on her own early stardom:

> *Just as a Hollywood pin-up represents sex to dissatisfied erotics, so I represented the ideal daughter millions of fathers and mothers wished they had.*

Clark Gable of Jean Harlow:

> *She didn't want to be famous. She wanted to be happy.*

Ernest Hemingway of Marlene Dietrich:

> *If she had nothing but her voice, she could break your heart with it. But she also has that beautiful body and the timeless loveliness of her face.*

Hedy Lamarr:

> *Any girl can be glamorous: all you have to do is stand still and look stupid.*

Marilyn Monroe:

> *A sex symbol becomes a thing. I hate being a thing.*

Sophia Loren:

> *Sex appeal is fifty per cent what you've got and fifty per cent what people think you've got.*

Spencer Tracy of Jean Harlow:

> *A square shooter if ever there was one.*

Rita Hayworth:

> *Every man I knew had fallen in love with Gilda and wakened with me.*

Greta
Garbo (1905-   )

*Boiled down to essentials, she is a plain mortal girl
with large feet.*

So wrote Herbert Kretzmer, sick of the 'sphinx' image, which
in the early thirties was overpowering. Alistair Cooke called
her:

*Every man's harmless fantasy mistress. She gave you
the impression that, if your imagination had to sin,
it could at least congratulate itself on its impeccable
taste.*

To Clare Boothe Luce she was:

*A deer in the body of a woman, living resentfully in
the Hollywood zoo.*

A 1929 critic said:

*She is a woman who marches to some unstruck
music, unheard by the rest of us.*

Rouben Mamoulian thought her:

A wonderful instrument.

Even the sensible Lillian Gish considered that:

*Garbo's temperament reflected the rain and gloom
of the long dark Swedish winters.*

More recently Ken Tynan remarked:

> *What when drunk one sees in other women, one
> sees in Garbo sober.*

Remoteness was part of her charm. To Fredric March:

> *Co-starring with Garbo hardly constituted an intro-
> duction.*

To James Wong Howe, the famous cameraman:

> *She was like a horse on the track. Nothing, and then
> the bell goes, and something happens.*

But the image always had its knockers, including the lady
herself:

> *I never said, I want to be alone. I only said I want
> to be* let *alone.*

(She did say it actually, but in *Grand Hotel*.) She added:

> *My talent falls within definite limits. I'm not a
> versatile actress.*

She also said with a smile:

> *I'm a woman who's unfaithful to a million men.*

But the fact is, men were not her fans. It was women who
queued to see her suffer. J. Robert Rubin of MGM noted
in wonder:

> *Garbo was the only one we could kill off. The
> Shearer and Crawford pictures had to end in a
> church, but the public seemed to enjoy watching
> Garbo die.*

In the seventies, thirty years after her retirement, her movies
were still making money all over the world and the lady herself
was front page news. You can't kill a legend. And it wasn't the
movies that kept the interest; as Richard Whitehall remarked:

> *Subtract Garbo from most of her films, and you are
> left with nothing.*

84

Samuel Goldwyn (1882-   )

He was the archetypal movie mogul: the glove salesman from Minsk who became more American than apple pie and founded his credo on the family audience. His maxims included:

> *Motion pictures should never embarrass a man when he brings his wife to the theatre.*

and:

> *I seriously object to seeing on the screen what belongs in the bedroom.*

He was proud of his art:

> *The picture makers will inherit the earth.*

As an executive, he certainly knew his own mind:

> *A producer shouldn't get ulcers: he should give them.*

and:

> *I was always an independent, even when I had partners.*

and:

> *In this business it's dog eat dog, and nobody's going to eat me.*

He was a great showman:

What we want is a story that starts with an earth-quake and works its way up to a climax...

But his logic was all his own:

I don't care if it doesn't make a nickel. I just want every man, woman and child in America to see it!

That was about *The Best Years of Our Lives*. Then there was the time he was stuck for a strong male lead and rang David Selznick:

David, we're both in terrible trouble. You've got Gable and I want him.

He disdained subtlety. When a harassed publicist devised a campaign that began:

The directing skill of Rouben Mamoulian, the radiance of Anna Sten and the genius of Samuel Goldwyn have combined to bring you the world's greatest entertainment...

Goldwyn nodded approval:

That's the kind of advertising I like. Just the facts. No exaggeration...

Did he really coin all the famous Goldwynisms which have filled so many books? Not all of them, perhaps. One doubts the authenticity of:

Directors are always biting the hand that lays the golden egg.

and:

In two words: im-possible,

and:

Tell me, how did you love the picture?

and:

We have all passed a lot of water since then.

But I imagine Goldwyn probably did say, rather wittily:

Gentlemen, kindly include me out.

and:

Let's bring it up to date with some snappy nine-teenth century dialogue.

and:

Anyone who goes to a psychiatrist should have his head examined.

and:

I had a great idea this morning, but I didn't like it.

and:

A verbal contract isn't worth the paper it's written on.

His film appreciation was untutored but vivid, like his speaking style:

When everybody's happy with the rushes, the picture's always a stinker,

he once said; and he can't have been alone among Hollywood producers in vowing:

I'd hire the devil himself if he'd write me a good story.

D. W. Griffith
(1874-1948)

He was the first to photograph thought.

said Cecil B. De Mille. It was quite a compliment. But Griffith was full of contradictions. His brain was progressive, his emotions Victorian. For a few years the two aspects were able to join in public favour, but he could not adapt himself to the brisker pace of the twenties, when he made many such blinkered and stubborn pronouncements as:

> *We do not want now and we never shall want the human voice with our films.*

He could be tactless too, as when in 1918 he commented:

> *Viewed as drama, the war is somewhat disappointing.*

Yet this was the man of whom Gene Fowler could say:

> *He articulated the mechanics of cinema and bent them to his flair.*

Lillian Gish, a great admirer of Griffith, said :

> *He inspired in us his belief that we were working in a medium that was powerful enough to influence the whole world.*

To Mack Sennett:

> *He was my day school, my adult education program, my university...(but) he was an extremely difficult man to know.*

He said himself:

The task I'm trying to achieve above all is to make you see...

He knew his own value, as many an actor found when asking for a raise:

It's worth a lot more than money to be working for me!

This was true enough up to the time of *The Birth of a Nation*, which President Wilson described as:

Like writing history with lightning.

But it became less so after the box-office flop of *Intolerance*, which Gene Fowler called:

The greatest commercial anticlimax in film history.

He became an embarrassment to Hollywood because his ideas seemed outmoded; in the thirties he scarcely worked at all. When he died in 1948 Hedda Hopper, recalling the marks made by stars in the wet cement at Hollywood's Chinese Theatre, said:

Griffith's footprints were never asked for, yet no one has ever filled his shoes...

And James Agee added:

There is not a man working in movies, nor a man who cares for them, who does not owe Griffith more than he owes anyone else.

Katharine
Hepburn (1909-)

The screen's first lady has never had a lot to say for herself.
Her most thoughtful piece of self-analysis was:

> *I was fortunate to be born with a set of charac-*
> *teristics that were in the public vogue.*

Cecil Beaton was more poetic than kind in his description:

> *She has a face that belongs to the sea and the wind,*
> *with large rocking-horse nostrils and teeth that you*
> *just know bite an apple every day.*

Robert Hopkins said of her physical angularity:

> *You could throw a hat at her, and wherever it hit, it*
> *would stick.*

Tennessee Williams thought her a dream actress:

> *She makes dialogue sound better than it is by a*
> *matchless clarity and beauty of diction, and by a*
> *fineness of intelligence and sensibility that illumin-*
> *ates every shade of meaning in every line she speaks.*

One feels too that she brings similar high standards to every
corner of her life. She said of herself:

> *When I started out, I didn't have any desire to be*
> *an actress or to learn how to act. I just wanted to*
> *be famous.*

Perhaps only chance kept her from being the first woman

president. She obviously has the charm, as Garson Kanin says:

As the years go by she does not lose her old admirers,
she goes on gaining new ones.

NO DON JUAN!
Women's adoration
leaves him cold —
but he uses it for his
mysterious purpose.

WILLIAM
POWELL
in
"Ladies'
Man"

A Paramount Picture
with
CAROLE LOMBARD
KAY FRANCIS

1931

Charlton Heston (1923-)

A careful and successful actor, Heston has been blessed with the kind of impressive face and physique that inevitably got him cast as a succession of epic heroes. This was a mixed blessing to his career. On one hand, as he said:

> *There's a special excitement in playing a man who made a hole in history large enough to be remembered centuries after he died.*

Commercially, furthermore:

> *If you can't make a career out of two de Milles, you'll never do it.*

On the other hand:

> *After spending all of last winter in armour it's a great relief to wear costume that bends.*

Heston has continued to explore, without having to resort to character parts. He knows however that:

> *The minute you feel you have given a faultless performance is the time to get out.*

Alfred
Hitchcock (1899-)

Hitch has not even had to build up his own legend: eager
critics like Truffaut have done it for him. The suspense master
has however obliged the press with a variety of *bon mots* about
himself and his work. Personally I like best his story of how he
caused consternation in a crowded elevator by muttering very
audibly to a friend:

> *I didn't think the old man would bleed so much.*

His little epigrams include:

> *Drama is life with the dull bits left out.*

and:

> *Always make the audience suffer as much as
> possible.*

and:

> *There is no terror in a bang, only in the anticipation
> of it.*

and:

> *Terror is a matter of surprise; suspense, of fore-
> warning.*

And his defence if the tricks don't work:

> *All things considered, I think I'm doing well if I get
> sixty per cent of my original conception on the
> screen.*

He despised long dialogue sequences:

> *A film maker isn't supposed to say things. He's supposed to show them.*

He despised actors too. One of his most widely publicised remarks was:

> *Actors are cattle.*

His current star, Carole Lombard, promptly led a troop of oxen onto the shooting stage and herself headed for home. Hitch thought it discreet to tell the press:

> *I didn't say actors are cattle. What I said was, actors should be treated like cattle.*

He clearly knows himself to be typecast as a mystery man:

> *If I made Cinderella, the audience would be looking out for a body in the coach.*

Perhaps his most quoted admission is:

> *That was the ending I wanted for Blackmail, but I had to change it for commercial reasons.*

Many tributes have been paid to him, but John Frankheimer's is all-embracing:

> *Any American director who says he hasn't been influenced by him is out of his mind.*

Doggedly into his seventies he continued to invent mayhem:

> *When people say I'm seventy I say that's a confounded lie. I'm twice 35, that's all. Twice 35.*

Hollywood

The legendary film city – sometimes referred to as Sodom-by-
the-Sea – seems far from glamorous to the casual visitor.
Geographically, it is not a city at all but a mere suburban seg-
ment of a forty-mile-square jigsaw puzzle of dormitory areas
which all run into each other. James Gleason, Dorothy Parker,
and several other people are credited with calling Los Angeles:

> *Seventy-two suburbs in search of a city.*

No matter who said it, it's still true. L.A. also remains a
supreme example of man's inhumanity to man, the promised
land that only humans have polluted. Even before the glorious
climate was filtered through several layers of smog, the values
were all wrong. The residents were almost all on the run from
somewhere else, and tended to idle their lives away under the
sun, pursuing the buck when they could and taking the biggest
for the best. Ethel Barrymore's first impressions, in 1932, were
vivid:

> *The people are unreal. The flowers are unreal, they
> don't smell. The fruit is unreal, it doesn't taste of
> anything. The whole place is a glaring, gaudy,
> nightmarish set, built up in the desert.*

The heat, the richness and the sweet smells are certainly ener-
vating. Shirley Maclaine, hot from Broadway, saw the difference at once:

> *The most important deals in the movie industry
> are finalised on the sun-drenched turf of golf courses
> or around turquoise swimming pools, where the
> smell of barbecue sauce is borne on gentle breezes
> and wafts over the stereo system of houses that
> people seldom leave.*

95

Cedric Hardwicke felt the danger:

> *God felt sorry for actors, so he gave them a place in the sun and a swimming pool. The price they had to pay was to surrender their talent.*

There's always a price tag. Fred Allen knew it when he said:

> *California is a great place...if you happen to be an orange.*

Someone else called it 'Siberia with palms'. Raymond Chandler aptly summed up L.A. as:

> *A city with all the personality of a paper cup.*

Joe Frisco thought of it as:

> *the only town in the world where you can wake up in the morning and listen to the birds coughing in the trees.*

Stephen Vincent Benet was even more picturesque:

> *Of all the Christbitten places in the two hemispheres, this is the last curly kink in the pig's tail.*

Hollywood is superior to other parts of L.A. only by virtue of the dusty hills into which it nestles on its northern side. The fact that most comments on it are cynical seems inevitable in an industrial area where the product is an intangible dream. Human beings must get injured in the process, their souls bruised by the struggle for fame, their bodies tossed onto the junkheap the minute they pass their prime. Hollywood has always sought, and then misused, the services of great talent. In the early thirties so many New York actors and writers made the four-day train journey and shortly returned in dejection that a saying sprang up on Broadway:

> *Never buy anything in Hollywood that you can't put on the Chief.*

Billie Burke, a longtime resident, declared that:

> *To survive there, you need the ambition of a Latin-American revolutionary, the ego of a grand opera tenor, and the physical stamina of a cow pony.*

Moss Hart called Beverly Hills:

> *The most beautiful slave quarters in the world.*

Nelson Algren had a brief but unhappy experience:

> *I went out there for a thousand a week, and I worked Monday and I got fired Wednesday. The fellow who hired me was out of town Tuesday.*

Walter Pidgeon liked the system:

> *It was like an expensive, beautifully-run fan club. You didn't need to carry money. Your face was your credit card — all over the world.*

But Dorothy Parker saw its dangers:

> *Hollywood money isn't money. It's congealed snow.*

Hedda Hopper put it another way:

> *Our town worships success, the bitch goddess whose smile hides a taste for blood.*

Ben Hecht couldn't even pretend to himself that he deserved his luck:

> *Hollywood held the lure...tremendous sums of money for work that required no more effort than a game of pinochle.*

John Huston also saw through the illusion:

> *Hollywood has always been a cage...a cage to catch our dreams.*

George Jean Nathan gave the most all-embracing description:

Ten million dollars worth of intricate and ingenious machinery functioning elaborately to put skin on baloney.

Oscar Levant was bitter:

Strip the phony tinsel off Hollywood and you'll find the real tinsel underneath.

Wilson Mizner thought it:

A trip through a sewer in a glass-bottomed boat,

and varied this thought as:

A sewer with service from the Ritz Carlton.

Dudley Field Malone found it:

A town where inferior people have a way of making superior people feel inferior.

To Grover Jones it was:

The only asylum run by the inmates.

Walter Winchell called it:

A town that has to be seen to be disbelieved.

And Marlon Brando dismissed it as:

A cultural boneyard.

Ken Murray loved it, but admitted it to be:

A place where you spend more than you make, on things you don't need, to impress people you don't like.

Ethel Barrymore was finally repelled:

> *It looks, it feels, as though it had been invented by*
> *a Sixth Avenue peepshow man.*

And Sonny Fox summed it all up:

> *Hollywood is like a world's fair that's been up a year*
> *too long.*

All such remarks spring mainly from the system. But perhaps
the people were partly to blame.

> *I'll miss Hollywood. Of the twenty friends I thought*
> *I had, I'll miss the six I really had,*

remarked Lauren Bacall wryly on her way to Broadway. And
Errol Flynn once said:

> *They've great respect for the dead in Hollywood,*
> *but none for the living.*

Richard Burton responded frankly to a question about Hollywood morals:

> *Certainly most movie executives were making love*
> *to starlets. But then, so were most of us actors.*

Alfred Hitchcock, on the other hand, maintained:

> *We lead a very suburban life here. We're in bed by*
> *nine o'clock every night.*

And that reminds one of the anonymous thirties complaint
about Hollywood's fabled social life:

> *No matter how hot it gets during the day, there's*
> *nothing to do at night.*

Anonymous too was the mogul-hater who averred:

There's nothing wrong with the place, that six first-class funerals wouldn't cure.

Nepotism was of course rife. When Louis B. Mayer appointed his daughter's husband William Goetz to a key position at MGM, someone cracked:

The son-in-law also rises.

And Ogden Nash devised a famous couplet about the head of Universal:

Uncle Carl Laemmle
Has a very large faemmle.

Ethics were out, as Dorothy Parker knew:

The only – ism Hollywood believes in is plagiarism.

Glamour and insincerity gave it the atmosphere of a luxury liner, as someone said in the thirties:

I have this terrible apprehension that suddenly the boat is going to dock and I shall never see any of you again.

Phyllis Batelli called it:

A place where great-grandmothers dread to grow old.

And there's an old saying:

In Hollywood the eternal triangle consists of an actor, his wife and himself.

(There is another version which runs 'an actor, his wife and his agent'. Take your choice.) Walter Winchell thought:

They shoot too many pictures and not enough actors.

One can hardly be surprised that people are false when the movies themselves were sham for so many years. 'Authentic' locations were created on the spot. Carl Laemmle said:

> *A tree is a tree. A rock is a rock. So shoot it in Griffith Park.*

The producers naturally came to prefer their own imitations. Arthur Freed produced the Scottish fantasy *Brigadoon* on the MGM lot and defended himself by saying:

> *I went to Scotland and found nothing there that looks like Scotland.*

A wise saying of Hollywood's heyday, by David O. Selznick:

> *Nothing here is permanent. Once photographed, life here is ended.*

But the system had its rueful supporters. Orson Welles:

> *Hollywood's all right: it's the pictures that are bad.*

Raymond Chandler:

> *If my books had been any worse I should not have been invited to Hollywood, and if they had been any better I should not have come.*

An anonymous writer:

> *They ruin your stories. They trample on your pride. They massacre your ideas. And what do you get for it? A fortune.*

Typically, Hollywood was often ignorant of the talent it had bought. Bert Lahr didn't make it until his third trip, and said wryly:

> *If you want to be a success in Hollywood, be sure and go to New York.*

Richard Dyer McCann wrote truthfully:

> *The most familiar, solid, bedrock certainty in Hollywood is sudden change.*

Certainly, the town depended on fashion, and its well-set ways were in themselves a mere fashion. By 1956, David Selznick found the place to be:

> *Like Egypt, full of crumbled pyramids.*

Fred Allen had said in 1941 that:

> *Hollywood is a place where people from Iowa mistake each other for stars.*

In the fifties the mistake became pardonable: male leads were required to look less like matinee idols and more like the slob next door, or the fellow at the gas station. Humphrey Bogart was heard to remark:

> *I came out here with one suit and everybody said I looked like a bum. Twenty years later Marlon Brando comes out with only a sweat shirt and the town drools over him. That shows you how much Hollywood has progressed.*

Hollywood was desperate in the face of TV and better living standards. One trend followed another (see Trends): in the sixties, for instance, English actors became more fashionable than ever before, and Bob Hope quipped:

> *There'll always be an England, even if it's in Hollywood.*

Whether it finally succeeds or goes under, it has had a fair run, long enough to confound two doubting remarks of 1915, by Carl Laemmle:

> *I hope I didn't make a mistake coming out here.*

And D. W. Griffith:

It's a shame to take this country away from the rattle-snakes.

Perhaps the rattle-snakes are just biding their time.

Horror

Quiz
In which horror films were the following lines heard?

1 Listen to them...creatures of the night. What music they make!
2 An intellectual carrot – the mind boggles!
3 To new worlds of Gods and Monsters!
4 What we need is young blood...and brains...
5 I'm going to tear the skin from your body – bit by bit!
6 Hoi, have you got the wrong vampire!
7 There just isn't room for two doctors and two vampires in one small town...
8 Have a potato...
9 Get away from that lever – you'll blow us all to atoms!
10 I have here a collection of the world's most astounding horrors...
11 I never drink...wine...
12 It went for a little walk...
13 Just room for one inside, sir!
14 I know you have a civil tongue in your head – I sewed it there myself!
15 (Complete the following verse:)
      Even the man who is pure in heart
      And says his prayers by night
      ....
      And the moon is pure and bright!

1 The line is inseparable from the actor: Bela Lugosi in the 1930 version of *Dracula*.

2 Spoken by the reporter in *The Thing from Another World* (1952), when the scientists have explained what kind of 'thing' they are dealing with.

3 A lively toast by Ernest Thesiger as Dr Praetorius, the evil genius of *Bride of Frankenstein* (1935).

4 Mr Lugosi again, this time spoofing himself in *Abbott and Costello meet Frankenstein* (1948). As he speaks he is benignly patting the head of Costello, for whom he sees a use in the reactivation of the Frankenstein monster.

5 The trouble with this climax to *The Black Cat* (1934) is that one can hardly depict the realization of the threat. The speaker is Lugosi, the victim Boris Karloff. As usual in films called The Black Cat, the cat has nothing to do with the story.

6 The funniest line in that otherwise disappointing spoof *The Fearless Vampire Killers* (or *Dance of the Vampires*) (1968). Alfie Bass is a Jewish vampire, so naturally scoffs at the crucifix held out to ward him off.

7 Max Adrian as the impeccable bloodsucker in *Dr Terror's House of Horrors* (1967), expressing regret for despatching his young rival.

8 Ernest Thesiger in *The Old Dark House* (1932) presiding over a very miserable supper party. His other characteristic line in the same film was 'Have some gin: it's my only weakness', and this was carried over intact into *Bride of Frankenstein* three years later.

9 Why such a lever should exist in the laboratory of *Bride of Frankenstein* (1935) was never explained, but it made a fine dramatic climax. The speaker was Ernest Thesiger, but fans will recall that he was insufficiently persuasive.

10 Not *House of Wax* but *House of Frankenstein* (1944) which was originally due to be called *Chamber of Horrors*. The owner of the travelling freak show was George Zucco, despatched in the first reel by J. Carrol Naish.

11 Bela 'Dracula' Lugosi again. At the time he was more interested in the blood oozing from a prick in his victim's finger.

12 Another line carried over from one film to another. In *The Mummy* (1932) Bramwell Fletcher stammers it out when asked what has happened to the mummy, which has just driven him half-mad by coming to life. The same director, Karl Freund, later used it in *Mad Love* (1935), applied by a passer-by to a wax figure which apparently becomes mobile but has actually been replaced by the heroine.

13 In the first story in *Dead of Night* (1945), a convalescent sees from a window a hearse, the driver of which (Miles Malleson) makes this chilling observation. Leaving hospital, he is about to board a bus when the conductor makes the same remark. He waves it on, and sees it crash over an embankment.

14 From the sadder days of the horror film: Whit Bissell speaks to his creation in *Teenage Frankenstein* (1957).

15 'May become a wolf when the wolf bane blooms' declaimed with perfect emphasis by Maria Ouspenskaya in *The Wolf Man* (1941).

Impersonations

Quiz
The following people all existed. For what work were they best
known, and who portrayed them in what films?

 1 Violette Szabo
 2 Tom Gaddis
 3 Paris Singer
 4 Lady Gregory
 5 Mrs Leslie Carter
 6 W. C. Handy
 7 Frank B. Gilbreth
 8 Pierre Curie
 9 Alvin York
10 Morey Bernstein
11 Mary Shelley
12 James Doolittle
13 Odette Churchill
14 Barnes Wallis
15 Ernie Pyle
16 Polly Adler
17 Sol Hurok
18 William Friese-Greene
19 Paul Ehrlich
20 Marjorie Laurence

 1 Spy; Virginia McKenna; *Carve Her Name with Pride*
 2 Writer; Edmond O'Brien; *Bird Man of Alcatraz*
 3 Industrialist; Jason Robards; *Isadora*
 4 Writer and patron of the arts; Edith Evans; *Young Cassidy*
 5 Actress; Miriam Hopkins; *Lady with Red Hair*
 6 Composer; Nat King Cole; *St Louis Blues*
 7 Efficiency expert; Clifton Webb; *Cheaper by the Dozen*
 8 Research scientist; Walter Pidgeon; *Madame Curie*
 9 War hero; Gary Cooper; *Sergeant York*
10 Psychic experimenter; Louis Hayward; *The Search for Bridey Murphy*
11 Writer; Elsa Lanchester; *The Bride of Frankenstein*
12 Colonel; Spencer Tracy; *Thirty Seconds Over Tokyo*
13 Spy; Anna Neagle; *Odette*
14 Research scientist; Michael Redgrave; *The Dam Busters*
15 War correspondent; Burgess Meredith; *The Story of G.I. Joe*
16 Madam; Shelley Winters; *A House is Not a Home*
17 Impressario; David Wayne; *Tonight We Sing*
18 Inventor; Robert Donat; *The Magic Box*
19 Research scientist; Edward G. Robinson; *Dr Ehrlich's Magic Bullet*
20 Opera singer; Eleanor Parker; *Interrupted Melody*

Insults

A choice selection, from scripts and from life.

Tony Curtis, about having to make love to Marilyn Monroe:

> *It's like kissing Hitler.*

George Sanders to Anne Baxter in *All About Eve*:

> *That I should want you at all suddenly seems to me
> the height of improbability.*

Louis B. Mayer to Greta Garbo's agent:

> *Tell her that in America men don't like fat women.*

Monty Woolley to Mary Wickes in *The Man Who Came to
Dinner*:

> *You have the touch of a sex-starved cobra.*

Mabel Normand at a press conference:

> *Say anything you like, but don't say I love to work.
> That sounds like Mary Pickford, that prissy bitch.*

Fredric March to Walter Connolly in *Nothing Sacred*:

> *The hand of God reaching down into the mire
> couldn't elevate you to the depths of degradation.*

And in the same movie, Walter Connolly to Fredric March:

> *I am sitting here, Mr Cook, toying with the idea*

of cutting out your heart and stuffing it – like an olive!

Billy Wilder, after listening to Cliff Osmond singing for a part:

You have Van Gogh's ear for music.

Jan Sterling to Kirk Douglas in *Ace in the Hole*:

I've met a lot of hard-boiled eggs in my time, but you – you're twenty minutes!

Boris
Karloff (1887-1969)

When I was nine I played the demon king in Cinderella and it launched me on a long and happy life of being a monster.

Though Karloff fought against being typecast, he later admitted:

The monster was the best friend I ever had.

How did he get the part? Said producer Carl Laemmle junior:

His eyes mirrored the suffering we needed.

Director James Whale amplified this:

His face fascinated me. I made drawings of his head, adding sharp bony ridges where I imagined the skull might have joined.

Karloff however insisted:

You could heave a brick out of the window and hit ten actors who could play my parts. I just happened to be on the right corner at the right time.

Charles
Laughton (1900-62)

*You can't direct a Laughton picture. The best you
can hope for is to referee.*

So said Alfred Hitchcock, who ought to know. This may have
been the reason for the sharp decline of a brilliant and
apparently diffident actor once he got to believe his own publicity. He said once:

*It's got so that every time I walk into a restaurant
I get not only soup but an impersonation of Captain
Bligh.*

He enjoyed it. He also said:

*The most beautiful thing of all is the complete still-
ness of an audience so intent that it hardly breathes.*

Intent on him, that is. Alexander Korda once complained that
Laughton would only act when he was in the mood:

*With him acting was an act of childbirth. What he
needed was not so much a director as a midwife.*

Alva Johnson called him:

*A great man who only accidentally became an
actor.*

It's a pity he wasn't happy in the part.

Stan Laurel (1890-1965) and Oliver Hardy (1892-1957)

They were visual comedians, of course. But they successfully transferred to sound by the use of minimum sound, mainly in the form of carefully scattered catch phrases which arose naturally out of their characters as every child's foolish uncles. When disaster struck, as it inevitably did, who could resist the sight of Olly among the debris, gazing reprovingly at the unharmed Stan and saying:

> *Here's* another *fine mess you've gotten me into.*

Or:

> *Why don't you do something to* help *me?*

Or simply:

> *I have* nothing *to say.*

Such results are Olly's reward for listening to Stan's suggestions earlier on. Stan's meaning is always unclear to begin with, so that Olly has to say:

> *Tell me that again.*

But he finally gets the drift and agrees:

> *That's a* good idea.

Olly of course was always shy, especially with women. When introduced, he was apt to twiddle his tie and observe:

> *A lot of weather we've been having lately.*

113

His great asset was his courtly manner, preserved even when mistaking an open can of milk for the telephone receiver:

Pardon me for a moment, my ear is full of milk.

Stan, having no catch phrases, relied on lively non sequiturs. When asked:

You never met my wife, did you?

He would reply:

Yes, I never did.

His speciality was putting his foot in it, as when he visits Olly in hospital and announces:

I brought you some hard boiled eggs and some nuts.

Not surprisingly, he eats them himself, having thoughtfully brought salt and pepper canisters in his pocket. Then there was the time in a bar when they could afford only one beer, ordered by Olly with his usual majesty. Stan did rather ruin the effect by calling after the waiter:

And two clean straws that haven't been used...

But he was capable of saying the right thing, as when Olly prepared a mundane repast of coffee and beans. Stan liked it:

Boy, you sure know how to plan a meal!

Behind the scenes, Stan was the producer. Olly was ready to admit:

I have never really worked hard in the creation department.

But he astutely saw the secret of their success:

Those two fellows we created, they were nice, very

nice people. They never get anywhere because they are both so dumb, but they don't know they're dumb. One of the reasons why people like us, I guess, is because they feel superior to us.

That was put another way in the opening title to one of their silent films:

Neither Mr Laurel nor Mr Hardy had any thoughts of getting married. In fact, they had no thoughts of any kind...

And the opening of *Come Clean* summed up their best comedy style very neatly:

Mr Hardy holds that a man should always tell his wife the whole truth.
Mr Laurel is crazy too.

THE SCREEN'S FIRST MUSICAL COMEDY

1929

Ernst
Lubitsch (1892-1947)

It's the Lubitsch touch that means so much

piped the posters.

He was the only director in Hollywood who had his own signature.

said S. N. Behrman. These were two ways of saying that Lubitsch was a master of cinematic innuendo.

I let the audience use their imaginations. Can I help it if they misconstrue my suggestions?

he asked archly. In fact he delighted in naughtiness, and carried it off with great delicacy, though he admitted his lapses:

I sometimes make pictures which are not up to my standard, but then it can only be said of a mediocrity that all his work is up to his standard.

The Marx Brothers:
Groucho (1891-)
Chico (1886-1961)
Harpo (1888-1964)
Zeppo (1896-)

The leader wore a large painted moustache and affected a cigar, and his three henchmen impersonated respectively a mute harpist afflicted with satyriasis, a larcenous Italian, and a jaunty coxcomb, who carried the love interest. — S. J. Perelman.

Lines written by or for the Marx Brothers would fill a book in themselves. This is a selection of personal favourites, arranged chronologically and attributed to the authors of the films concerned.

1929: *The Cocoanuts* (George S. Kaufman, Morrie Ryskind)

Ah, Mrs Rittenhouse, won't you...lie down?

I'll wrestle anybody in the crowd for five dollars.

Be free, my friends. One for all and all for me — me for you and three for five and six for a quarter.

Do you know that this is the biggest development since Sophie Tucker?

Your eyes shine like the pants of my blue serge suit.

1930: *Animal Crackers* (George S. Kaufman and Morrie Ryskind)

You're the most beautiful woman I've ever seen, which doesn't say much for you.

What do you get an hour?

117

– For playing, we get ten dollars an hour.
What do you get for not playing?
– Twelve dollars an hour. Now for rehearsing, we make a special rate – fifteen dollars an hour.
And what do you get for not rehearsing?
– You couldn't afford it. You see, if we don't rehearse, we don't play. And if we don't play, that runs into money.
How much would you want to run into an open manhole?
– Just the cover charge.
Well, drop in some time.
– Sewer.
Well, I guess we cleaned that up.

You go Uruguay and I'll go mine.

One morning I shot an elephant in my pajamas. How he got into my pajamas I'll never know.

1931: *Monkey Business* (S. J. Perelman, Will B. Johnstone, Arthur Sheekman)

Do you want your nails trimmed long?
– Oh, about an hour and a half. I got nothing to do.

Look at me: I worked my way up from nothing to a state of extreme poverty.

I want to register a complaint. Do you know who sneaked into my room at three o'clock this morning?.........
– Who?......
Nobody, and that's my complaint.

Do you suppose I could buy back my introduction to you?

Sir, you have the advantage of me.
– Not yet I haven't, but wait till I get you outside.

1932: *Horse Feathers* (Bert Kalmar, Harry Ruby,
S. J. Perelman, Will B. Johnstone)

*Why don't you bore a hole in yourself and let the
sap run out?*

*There's a man outside with a big black moustache.
— Tell him I've got one.*

*The dean is furious. He's waxing wroth.
— Is Roth out there too? Tell Roth to wax the dean
for a while.*

*You're a disgrace to our family name of Wagstaff,
if such a thing is possible.*

*You've got the brain of a four-year-old boy, and I
bet he was glad to get rid of it.*

*What a day! Spring in the air!
— Who, me? I should spring in the air and fall in
the lake?*

1933: *Duck Soup* (Bert Kalmar, Harry Ruby,
Arthur Sheekman, Nat Perrin)

Take a card. You can keep it: I've got fifty-one left.

*My husband is dead.
— I'll bet he's just using that as an excuse.
I was with him to the end.
— No wonder he passed away.
I held him in my arms and kissed him.
— So it was murder!*

*This is a gala day for you.
— That's plenty. I don't think I could manage more
than one gal a day.*

*What is it that has four pairs of pants, lives in
Philadelphia, and it never rains but it pours?*

119

I could dance with you till the cows come home. On second thoughts I'll dance with the cows and you come home.

Excuse me while I brush the crumbs out of my bed. I'm expecting company.

1935: *A Night at the Opera* (George S. Kaufman, Morrie Ryskind, Al Boasberg)

Do they allow tipping on the boat?
— Yes, sir.
Have you got two fives?
— Oh, yes, sir.
Then you won't need the ten cents I was going to give you.

Let joy be unconfined. Let there be dancing in the streets, drinking in the saloons, and necking in the park.

1937: *A Day at the Races* (George Seaton, Robert Pirosh, George Oppenheimer)

She looks like the healthiest woman I ever met.
— You look like you never met a healthy woman.

Don't point that beard at me, it might go off.

Closer...hold me closer...
— If I hold you any closer I'll be in back of you!

Marry me and I'll never look at another horse.

Isn't that awfully large for a pill?
— Well, it was too small for a basketball and I didn't know what to do with it.

One dollar and you remember me all your life.
— That's the most nauseating proposition I've ever had.

1939: *At the Circus* (Irving Brecher)

> *If you hadn't sent for me, I'd be at home now in
> a comfortable bed with a hot toddy. – That's a
> drink!*

> *I bet your father spent the first year of your life
> throwing rocks at the stork.*

1945: *A Night in Casablanca* (Joseph Fields, Roland Kibbee,
Frank Tashlin)

> *The first thing we're going to do is change all the
> numbers on all the doors.
> – But sir, think of the confusion...
> Yeah, but think of the fun.*

> *Hey boss, you got a woman in there?
> – If I haven't, I've been wasting thirty minutes of
> valuable time.*

> *I'm Beatrice Ryner. I stop at the hotel.
> – I'm Ronald Kornblow. I stop at nothing.*

Groucho himself later proved to be sometimes as funny as his
scripts. He wrote to resign from a club:

> *I don't care to belong to any social organisation
> which would acept me as a member.*

And he wrote a threatening letter to Confidential magazine:

> *Dear Sir: If you continue to publish slanderous
> pieces about me I shall feel compelled to cancel my
> subscription.*

Louis B.
Mayer (1885-1957)

This 'Hollywood rajah' was perhaps the archetypal movie mogul: sentimental, commonsensical, businesslike, unaesthetic, arrogant, illogical, naïve, amoral, tasteless and physically unappealing. For twenty years he ran MGM splendidly in his own image, and became a legend of autocracy. He did not stint on his surroundings; Sam Goldwyn said of his office:

You need an automobile to reach the desk.

No detail escaped him. B. P. Schulberg gave him the title:

Czar of all the rushes.

Though he kept it well hidden, he did have a basic sense of humility:

You know how I'm smart? I got people around me who know more than I do.

His arguments were often irritatingly unanswerable. Arthur Freed recalls:

If a writer complained of his work being changed, Mayer always said:
'The number one book of the ages was written by a committee, and it was called The Bible.'

To Gottfried Reinhardt, who wanted to make a non-commercial picture, Mayer snapped:

You want to be an artist, but you want other people to starve for your art.

122

Mayer's idea of a good commercial movie was simple, home-spun, warm, happy...in a phrase, the Hardy Family. That series, cheap to make, kept the studio in profit for many a year. Their success did not delude Mayer into thinking they were great movies:

> *Don't make these pictures any better. Just keep them the way they are.*

This did not mean that he despised the American public, only that he knew what they liked. He even created and acted out for the producer a prayer that the son of the fictional family might speak when his mother was ill:

> *Dear God, don't let my mom die, because she's the best mom in the world.*

He was similarly quick to correct a plot point:

> *A boy may hate his father, but he will always respect him.*

As early as 1922 his credo in this vein was fully formed:

> *I will only make pictures that I won't be ashamed to have my children see.*

His cry in later years, when permissiveness was creeping in, was:

> *Don't show the natural functions!*

In argument Mayer was a great and exhausting opponent, violent, wheedling and pleading by turns. Robert Taylor remembered going in for more money. When he emerged, a friend asked him:

> *Did you get the raise?*
> *– No, but I gained a father.*

123

Mayer was very proud of MGM's army of stars and technicians:

We are the only kind of company whose assets all walk out of the gate at night.

He needed their goodwill:

I want to rule by love, not fear.

But when he died, the usual caustic comments were heard:

The only reason so many people attended his funeral was they wanted to make sure he was dead.

He had then been for some years at odds with the MGM hierarchy, an unwilling exile from the boardroom. Said someone at the funeral:

I see MGM got L.B. back at last.
– Yeah, but on its own terms.

Misnomers

A title has to appeal to the greatest possible number of people. Sometimes it loses its relevance in the progress; sometimes, as in metaphors like *Straw Dogs* and *A Clockwork Orange*, the film-maker is too arrogant to explain it. Here are one or two examples where the irrelevance is still traceable.

The Black Cat. Hardly any of the several films under this title have had much to do with Poe's story, and although a black cat may have casually strolled across the scene it has had little bearing on the plot. In Britain the 1934 version was re-titled *House of Doom*, which is a little more to the point of the story.

Son of Dracula, like many other horror films, soon proved to have an inapposite label: the protagonist is none other than the old Count himself in disguise. In *Bride of Frankenstein*, the title role is a minor one, played by Valerie Hobson; the real bride is that of the monster. In *Frankenstein Created Woman*, he doesn't: he merely performs some brain-switching. In *Abbott and Costello Meet Frankenstein*, the Baron doesn't appear at all: it's the monster they meet, and he has much less to do with the plot than Dracula or the Wolf Man.

Abbott and Costello were never careful about titles. In *Abbott and Costello go to Mars*, they go to Venus. And *Abbott and Costello meet the Killer, Boris Karloff* seems devised purely for equality of billing; it is doubly misleading, for not only is Boris Karloff not a killer, he does not even play a killer in the movie.

The original title *The Thin Man* referred to a minor character in the murder plot. As sequel followed sequel, and continuity had to be maintained, the tag gradually attached itself to the investigator played by William Powell.

The films of W. C. Fields were noted for the studied irrelevance of their titles, the crowning glory being *Never give a Sucker an Even Break*. Laurel and Hardy were not far behind, as anyone knows who has tried to explain the relevance of *Hog Wild, You're Darn Tootin', Be Big, Wrong Again, Double Whoopee* or *They Go Boom*. Woody Allen is plainly in the great tradition: when asked why he called his movie *Bananas*, he replied, 'because there are no bananas in it'.

The Glass Bottom Boat is seen in the first sequence of the film titled after it, but it is not essential to that sequence and has no relevance at all to the rest of the movie.

It Happened One Night. Which night? The film covers several, and none is central to the plot.

Big Deal at Dodge City is the British title for *Big Hand for a Little Lady*. It is not only less attractive but wildly inaccurate, as the action is clearly denoted as taking place in Laredo! It was the work of a title fiend operating in Warner's London office, who also turned *An American Dream* into the weirdly irrelevant *See You in Hell, Darling*.

Halls of Montezuma is set in the Pacific, and *To the Shores of Tripoli* never leaves a California training camp. All the titles tell you is that the characters are Marines, from whose marching song the labels are taken.

In *Northwest Passage*, the passage is barely mentioned and never explored. MGM started to film Kenneth Roberts' historical novel in 1939. The script was too long, so they decided to make two films, the first to deal with the training of Rogers' Rangers and the second with their exploits. The second film was never made; the one that exists does have a subtitle, 'Part One: Rogers' Rangers'.

The Silencers, Murderers Row, The Ambushers. Any reader who can link these Matt Helm titles to their plots deserves a small prize.

Marilyn
Monroe (1926-62)

The tragedy of Marilyn Monroe was such that she has inspired more books of reminiscence and analysis than any other star. Her problem was, oddly enough, best expressed in an earlier decade by Clara Bow:

> *Being a sex symbol is a heavy load to carry, especially when one is tired, hurt and bewildered.*

Monroe knew her own limitations:

> *To put it bluntly, I seem to be a whole superstructure with no foundation. But I'm working on the foundation.*

What she meant by that was:

> *The best way for me to prove myself as a person is to prove myself as an actress.*

She was uncertain whether she would ever achieve this aim. She said once:

> *I enjoy acting when you really hit it right.*

But she seldom felt she did. In her search for meaning she married playwright Arthur Miller, and the headline was

EGGHEAD WEDS HOURGLASS

It finally failed to work although he was kind to her with press comments such as:

> *Her beauty shines because the spirit is forever showing itself.*

127

Not that she was lacking in moral supporters; even unlikely people such as Edith Sitwell acclaimed her:

> *She knows the world, but this knowledge has now lowered her great and benevolent dignity; its darkness has not dimmed her goodness.*

She settled for a flip image as expressed in her lively encounters with the press:

> *Didn't you have anything on?*
> *— I had the radio on.*
>
> *Sex is part of nature, and I go along with nature.*
>
> *Do you wear falsies?*
> *— Those who know me better, know better.*

The contradictions within herself finally killed her, and the obituaries were many and varied:

> *You don't have to hold an inquest to find out who killed Marilyn Monroe. Those bastards in the big executive chairs killed her.*
> *— Henry Hathaway*
>
> *If she was simple it would have been easy to help her. She could have made it with a little luck.*
> *— Arthur Miller*
>
> *A professional amateur.*
> *— Laurence Olivier*
>
> *Directing her was like directing Lassie. You needed fourteen takes to get each one of them right.*
> *— Otto Preminger*
>
> *Anyone can remember lines, but it takes a real artist to come on the set and not know her lines and give the performance she did.*
> *— Billy Wilder*

128

I have never met anyone as utterly mean as Marilyn Monroe. Nor as utterly fabulous on the screen, and that includes Garbo.
— *Billy Wilder*

As near genius as any actress I ever knew.
— *Joshua Logan*

She was born afraid. She never got over it. In the end fear killed her.
— *Pete Martin*

Anchor Here!

why
sailors
come home!

**CLARA
BOW**
IN 'True to
the Navy"
A Paramount Picture

Gobs of Love!
And Clara sings
"There's Only
One Who Mat-
ters"!

1930

Monsters

What monster:

1 Gobbled up Cecil Kellaway in a bathysphere?
2 Tickled Fay Wray's tummy?
3 Hung Dwight Frye?
4 Turned into Matt Dillon?
5 Had Claude Rains for a father?
6 Fell in love with Zita Johann?
7 Abducted Anne Bancroft?
8 Obeyed Roddy Macdowall?
9 Electrocuted Lionel Atwill?
10 Had lunch with Ernest Thesiger?
11 Met his doom in Westminster Abbey?
12 Spelt his name backwards?
13 Shot at his own reflection in a room full of mirrors?
14 Sought a flower called *Mariphasa Lupina*?
15 Was played by Carol's Reed's nephew?
16 Lived on Metaluna?
17 Menaced Jane Randolph in a swimming bath?
18 Lost her head to Christopher Lee?
19 Was cured by Onslow Stevens?
20 Caught up with Niall MacGinnis on a railway line?

Answers

1 *The Beast from 20,000 Fathoms* (1948).
2 *King Kong* (1933).
3 The monster in *Frankenstein* (1931).
4 *The Thing From Another World* (1952) – who was played by James Arness.
5 Lon Chaney Junior as *The Wolf Man* (1940).
6 Boris Karloff as *The Mummy* (1932).
7 The nameless actor who played the *Gorilla at Large* (1954).
8 The Golem in *It* (1957).
9 Lon Chaney Junior as the electric man in *Man Made Monster* (1941).
10 Boris Karloff as the monster in *Bride of Frankenstein*, (1935).
11 Richard Wordsworth as the outcome of *The Quatermass Experiment* (1955).
12 Lon Chaney Junior, who in *Son of Dracula* (1942) turned up in America as Count Alucard; or Christopher Lee, who borrowed the trick in *Dracula A.D. 1972.*
13 Boris Karloff in *The Raven* (1935).
14 Henry Hill or Warner Oland in *Werewolf of London* (1935).
15 The hero of *Curse of the Werewolf* (1962) (Oliver Reed).
16 The mutant in *This Island Earth* (1955).
17 Simone Simon in her cat form in *Cat People* (1942).
18 *The Gorgon* (1964); he beheaded her.
19 Lon Chaney Jnr as the wolf man in *House of Dracula* (1945).
20 The demon in *Night of the Demon* (1957).

Movies

The cinema is an art. Movies are...well, movies. Are they a good thing? To Cecil B. de Mille they were:

The new literature.

To Barbra Streisand, starting to shoot *Funny Girl*:

This is for posterity. Everything I do will be on film forever.

To Sarah Bernhardt they were:

My one chance for immortality.

Darryl F. Zanuck called them:

The greatest political fact in the world today.

Sam Spiegel was careful in his commendation:

The best motion pictures are those which reach you as entertainment, and by the time you leave have provoked thoughts. A picture that provokes no thoughts is usually not well conceived and does not entertain one anyway.

Warren Beatty gave a verbal shrug:

Movies are fun, but they're not a cure for cancer.

Ben Hecht took the money and ran:

Movies are one of the bad habits that have cor-
rupted our century.

and:

They have slipped into the American mind more
misinformation in one evening than the Dark Ages
could muster in a decade.

and:

A movie is never any better than the stupidest man
connected with it.

David O. Selznick was thoughtful:

There might have been good movies if there had
been no movie industry.

St John Ervine had little time for them:

American movies are written by the half-educated
for the half-witted.

H. L. Mencken similarly called them:

Entertainment for the moron majority.

And added:

The kind of jackass who likes the movies as they
are is the kind who keeps them as they are.

Robert E. Sherwood was scathing in 1922:

Who invented hokum? Think how much money
he'd have made from the film producers if he'd
sold his invention on a royalty basis!

Will Rogers was satirical:

133

There's only one thing that can kill the movies, and that's education.

Maybe Robert Mitchum has the last word:

What's history going to say about the movies? All those rows of seats facing a blank screen? Crazy!

Meanwhile, a few tips on the making of movies:

Whoever has the original idea for a film, it is soon taken away from him.
— *Ivan Butler*

You should think of each shot as you make it as the most important one in the film.
— *Henry Blanke*

Don't act, think!
— *F. W. Murnau*

Editing is crucial. Imagine James Stewart looking at a mother nursing a child. You see the child, then cut back to him. He smiles. Now Mr Stewart is a benign old gentleman. Take away the middle piece of film and substitute a girl in a bikini. Now he's a dirty old man.
— *Alfred Hitchcock*

Making a film is like going down a mine — once you've started you bid a metaphorical goodbye to the daylight and the outside world for the duration.
— *John Schlesinger*

In a good movie, the sound could go off and the audience would still have a perfectly clear idea of what was going on.
— *Alfred Hitchcock*

Nicknames

Quiz

For affectionate or other reasons, many stars have had nick-
names attached to them by publicists or journalists. How many
of these people can you recognise?

 1 The Body
 2 The It Girl
 3 The Oomph Girl
 4 The Biograph Girl
 5 The Peekaboo Girl
 6 The Love Rouser
 7 The Fiddle and the Bow
 8 America's Sweetheart
 9 The Sex Kitten
10 The Threat
11 The Great Profile
12 The Platinum Blonde
13 The Viennese Teardrop
14 The Clothes Horse
15 The Iron Butterfly
16 The Singing Capon
17 King of the Cowboys
18 The Man You Love to Hate
19 The Master
20 The Beard
21 The Man of a Thousand Faces
22 The Magnificent Wildcat
23 The First Lady of the Screen
24 The Empress of Emotion
25 The Duke
26 The World's Greatest Actor

1 Marie McDonald
2 Clara Bow
3 Ann Sheridan
4 Florence Lawrence
5 Veronica Lake (from her hair-do which covered one eye)
6 Buddy Rogers (in 1928)
7 Laurel and Hardy
8 Mary Pickford
9 Brigitte Bardot
10 Lizabeth Scott
11 John Barrymore
12 Jean Harlow
13 Luise Rainer
14 Joan Crawford
15 Jeanette Macdonald
16 Nelson Eddy
17 Tom Mix
18 Erich Von Stroheim
19 D. W. Griffith, or (more in the theatre) Noel Coward
20 Monty Woolley
21 Lon Chaney Senior
22 Pola Negri
23 Norma Shearer
24 Elissa Landi
25 John Wayne
26 John Barrymore (especially for *Don Juan*, 1927)
27 Lon Chaney Junior
28 George Arliss
29 Clark Gable
30 Francis X. Bushman

Mary
Pickford (1893-   )

The appeal of the world's sweetheart is not well understood in
the seventies. Her screen image was ever-childlike, sweet and
demure, the antithesis of today's heroines. Alistair Cooke said:

> *She was the girl every young man wanted to have –*
> *as his sister.*

Yet on first encounter D. W. Griffith told her:

> *You're too little and too fat, but I might give you*
> *a job.*

Later, he ruefully recollected:

> *She never stopped listening and learning.*

She was soon telling Adolph Zukor:

> *I can't afford to work for only ten thousand dollars*
> *a week.*

And Sam Goldwyn reflected:

> *It took longer to make one of Mary's contracts than*
> *it did to make one of Mary's pictures.*

Spoiled by success she may have been, but never blind to her
own failings:

> *I never liked one of my pictures in its entirety.*

Richard Griffith and Arthur Mayer thought the secret of her
success was that:

Her sweetness and light were tempered by a certain realism. In spite of her creed, the Glad Girl knew it was no cinch to make everything come out right. Nothing could have been more in tune with an era which combined limitless optimism with a belief that 'git up and git' was necessary to make optimism come true.

1932

Pseudonyms

Quiz

Who was also known as

1 Sleep'n Eat?
2 William B. Goodrich?
3 Parkyakarkus?
4 Billie Cassin?
5 Diane Belmont?
6 Bryant Fleming?
7 Blade Stanhope Conway?
8 Joseph Walton?
9 Stephen Richards?
10 Bettina Dawes?
11 Robert Rich?
12 Emily Clark, Harriet Brown, Jane Emerson, Gussie Berger, Mary Holmquist, Karin Lund?
13 John Elder, Henry Younger?
14 Mark Canfield?
15 Mahatma Kane Jeeves?

1 Willie Best

2 Fatty Arbuckle, when he attempted a comeback after the scandal which blighted his career.

3 Harry Einstein, a New York comedian of the thirties.

4 Joan Crawford

5 Lucille Ball

6 Gig Young

7 Robert Cummings, when posing as an Englishman.

8 Joseph Losey, when the McCarthy witch-hunt prevented him from working in England. This is the name under which he directed *The Intimate Stranger*.

9 Mark Stevens

10 Bette Davis, very briefly when first signed by Warners.

11 Dalton Trumbo, who under this name in 1956 received an Academy Award for the story of *The Brave One* at a time when he was officially blacklisted after the McCarthy witch-hunt.

12 These are all names used by Greta Garbo when travelling 'incognito'.

13 Anthony Hinds and Michael Carreras, when writing scripts for their own Hammer horror films.

14 Darryl F. Zanuck when writing screenplays.

15 W. C. Fields when writing screenplays.

Publicity

Quiz

No right-minded film-maker believes his own publicity...but he surely hopes it works. The tag-line devised for a film can have a make-or-break effect on its box-office record. Seldom can such lines be claimed as an honest distillation of truth, and very often they hint at more sensations than can be found in the film to which they are attached. But for sheer ingenuity some are unbeatable, and a few have even passed into the language.

The following lines have been grouped into decades. Which films did they puff?

The Seventies:
1. The story of a homosexual who married a nymphomaniac!
2. Hope never dies for a man with a good dirty mind!
3. They stand side by side. Young and old. Rich and poor. They gather together for a single purpose. *Survival.*
4. We don't love – we just make love. And damn little of that!
5. She gave away secrets to one side and her heart to the other!

The Sixties:
6. The motion picture with something to offend everybody!
7. Beware the beat of the cloth-wrapped feet!
8. The world's most uncovered undercover agent!
9. Don't give away the ending – it's the only one we have!
10. Every time a woman turns her face away because she's tired or unwilling, there's someone waiting like me...
11. A thousand thrills – and Hayley Mills!
12. A picture that goes beyond what men think about – because no man ever thought about it in quite this way!
13. The hot line suspense comedy!
14. You may not believe in ghosts, but you cannot deny terror...

15 You can expect the unexpected!
16 Now – add a motion picture to the wonders of the world!
17 One man...three women...one night!
18 £10,000 if you die of fright!
19 You'll laugh your pants off!
20 The picture with the fear flasher and the horror horn!
21 Meet the girls with the thermo-nuclear navels! The most tempting timebombs you've ever been tempted to trigger!
22 Keep the children home! And if you are squeamish, stay home with them!
23 A side of life you never expected to see on the screen!
24 You are cordially invited to George and Martha's for an evening of fun and games...
25 Why the crazy title? If we told you, you'd only laugh!

The Fifties:
26 Sing, Judy! Dance, Judy! The world is waiting for your sunshine!
27 Even in the first wild joy of her arms, he realised that she would be...an unfit mother!
28 A lion in your lap!
29 In making this film, MGM feel privileged to add something of permanent value to the cultural treasure house of mankind...
30 You have never really seen Gregory Peck until you see him in Cinemascope!
31 Their picture is not in the history books. It has never been seen on the screen – until now!
32 A hard cop and a soft dame...
33 A completely new experience between men and women!
34 He faced a decision that someday may be yours to make!
35 The colossus who conquered the world! The most colossal motion picture of all time!

The Forties:
36 You can't keep a good monster down!
37 A romantic gentleman by day – a love-mad beast by night!
38 The minx in mink with a yen for men!
39 The immortal thriller...
40 How'd you like to tussle with Russell?
41 Gable's back and Garson's got him!

42 No one is as good as Bette when she's bad!

43 There never was a woman like...

44 It tells *all* about those Brontë sisters!

45 More thrilling than the deeds of man...more beautiful than the love of woman...more wonderful than the dreams of children.

46 The picture they were born for!

47 The picture that helped to win the war!

48 He's as fast on the draw as he is in the drawing room!

49 We're going to see Jennifer Jones *again* in...

50 The sum total of all human emotions!

The Thirties:

51 Romance aflame through dangerous days and nights of terror! In a land where anything can happen – most of all to a beautiful girl alone!

52 The picture made behind locked doors!

53 The strangest love a man has ever known!

54 More sensational than her unforgettable father!

55 He's just as funny as his old man was fierce!

56 Three centuries in the making!

57 He plucked from the gutter a faded rose and made an immortal masterpiece!

58 135 women – with men on their minds!

59 He treated her rough – and she loved it!

60 A story so momentous it required six Academy Award stars and a cast of 1186 players!

61 Only the rainbow itself can duplicate its brilliance!

62 The shame of a nation!

63 A monster in form but human in his desire for love!

64 Boiling passions in the burning sands!

65 Six sticks of dynamite that blasted his way to freedom – and awoke America's conscience!

The Twenties:

66 The dangerous age for women is from three to seventy!

67 A photoplay of tempestuous love between a madcap English beauty and a bronzed Arab chief!

68 A cast of 125,000!

69 The mightiest dramatic spectacle of all the ages!

70 The epic of the American doughboy!

1 *The Music Lovers*, Ken Russell's fantasia on the life of Tschaikovsky.

2 This curious way to characterize a hero was devised for Peter Sellers in *Hoffman*.

3 Believe it or not: Chekov's *The Seagull*, Sidney Lumet version.

4 Richard Brooks' *The Happy Ending*: the new style 'woman's picture'.

5 Julie Andrews in *Darling Lili*, Blake Edwards' unsuccessful 'blockbuster'.

6 *The Loved One*, Tony Richardson's version of the Evelyn Waugh novel about bizarre burial practices in California.

7 *The Mummy's Shroud*. Probably tongue-in-cheek, but I wouldn't swear to it.

8 Who but Raquel Welch? The film was *Fathom*.

9 A Hitchcock ploy for *Psycho*.

10 A blurb which gave an entirely false picture of *The Dark at the Top of the Stairs*, a charming period family drama about a child's dawning awareness of sex. The title didn't help, either.

11 *In Search of the Castaways*.

12 Fellini's *Eight and a Half*.

13 *Dr Strangelove*.

14 *The Haunting*. One way to sell a ghost story in the rational 60s.

15 *Charade*.

16 Would you believe *Taras Bulba*?

17 Not a piece of European porn, but Tennessee Williams' *The Night of the Iguana*.

18 *Macabre*. Was anyone paid off?

19 A somewhat crude promise for the revival compilation *Laurel and Hardy's Laughing Twenties*.

20 An exploitation item called *Chamber of Horrors*: whenever a horror moment came up the audience was assailed with visual and aural warnings much more unnerving than the film itself.

21 *Dr Goldfoot and the Girl Bombs*.

22 *Witchfinder General*, known in America rather pointlessly as *The Conqueror Worm*.

23 *A Walk on the Wild Side*, Hollywood's first official visit to a brothel since the early thirties.

24 *Who's Afraid of Virginia Woolf?*

25 A rather desperate lure for *The Russians are Coming, the Russians are Coming!*

26 *A Star is Born*, which as a movie was *not* exactly sunny: and the world proved not to be waiting for the return of Miss Garland.

27 A Universal programmer called *Because of You*.

28 *Bwana Devil*, the first 3–D feature.

29 *Quo Vadis*. Yes, really.

30 *Night People*.

31 *Desiree*. (Marlon Brando as Napoleon.)

32 A titillating come on for *The Big Heat*.

33 *The Men*, Fred Zinnemann's film about paraplegics, who are paralysed from the waist down. The mind boggles...

34 Glenn Ford in *Ransom*: he played a wealthy man whose son was kidnapped.

35 *Alexander the Great*.

36 *The Ghost of Frankenstein*. Universal gave this sign that they had stopped taking their monsters seriously.

37 Spencer Tracy as *Dr Jekyll and Mr Hyde*.

38 *Lady in the Dark*, the first psychoanalysis comedy.

39 *Orpheus*.

40 Of course: *The Outlaw*. Catch-line allegedly by Howard Hughes.

41 A notorious tag for *Adventure*.

42 *In This Our Life*.

43 ...Gilda.

44 A rather flat little historical romance which distorted all the facts and personalities under the meaningless title *Devotion*. The publicity also included a reference to Thackeray (played by Sidney Greenstreet) as 'the furious fat man, the "friend" of the family...'

45 All this for Rudyard Kipling's *Jungle Book*.

46 True in a way: Bogart and Bacall in *The Big Sleep*.

47 This was applied to a reissue of *Mrs Miniver*.

48 A highly unsuitable come-on for *The Maltese Falcon*.

49 The insistent rhythm of this slogan for *The Song of Bernadette* drove Londoners mad throughout the last years of the war.

50 A forgettable melodrama called *Leave Her to Heaven.*
51 *Gunga Din*, a man's film if ever there was one. The entirely dispensable heroine was Joan Fontaine.
52 *Dr Cyclops.*
53 The way the Universal boys in 1930 sold what seemed like an absolute loser. The title was *Dracula.*
54 *Dracula's Daughter.*
55 *Son of Kong.* Its makers knew it was a poor imitation, so they played it as a comedy.
56 Warner's 1935 version of *A Midsummer Night's Dream.*
57 *The Life of Emile Zola.*
58 *The Women.*
59 *Red Dust.*
60 *Juarez.*
61 *The Adventures of Robin Hood,* which marked a genuine step forward in the use of Technicolor.
62 *Scarface.* The phrase was also used as an alternative title in some areas, to please the censor.
63 *Bride of Frankenstein.*
64 *The Lost Patrol.*
65 *I am a Fugitive from a Chain Gang.*
66 *Adam's Rib* (1922).
67 *The Sheik.*
68 The silent *Ben Hur.*
69 De Mille's *The Ten Commandments* (1923).
70 *The Big Parade.*

NB In 1972 a New York magazine ran a competition, inviting readers to invent way-out and hilarious tag-lines for non-existent movies. The results were hilarious, but not so way-out that one can't imagine them being snapped up and used pretty quickly. Here are some of the winners:

Makes Myra Breckinridge look like Snow White!

It took guts to film. Have you the guts to see it?

There were four men in her life. One to love her. One to marry her. One to take care of her. And one to kill her...

They lived a lifetime in 24 crowded hours!

The picture that could change your life – or save it!

If you scoff at the powers of darkness, do not see this film alone!

The book they said could never be written has become the movie they said could never be filmed!

Put Downs

Waspish comments about other people always make good reading. Here are a few for starters:

He looks as though his idea of fun would be to find a nice cold damp grave and sit in it.
— Richard Winnington of Paul Henried (1946)

A great showman who has never bothered to learn anything about making a movie...no one is more skilled at giving the appearance of dealing with large controversial themes in a bold way, without making the tactical error of doing so.
— Dwight Macdonald of Otto Preminger

Did you ever catch him at a funeral? It's wonderful. All through the years he makes notes on his friends. He wants to be ready.
— Eddie Cantor of George Jessel,
*   Hollywood's 'toastmaster general'*

He was a quaint artist who had no business in business.
— Mack Sennett of Harry Langdon

If that child had been born in the middle ages, she'd have been burned as a witch.
— Lionel Barrymore of Margaret O'Brien (1945)

Her friends always stand by her. When she prematurely published a claim that an actress was pregnant, the actress's husband hastened to prove her correct.
— Time magazine of Louella Parsons

149

He's the kind of guy that, when he dies, he's going up to heaven and give God a bad time for making him bald.
    — Marlon Brando of Frank Sinatra

Wet she was a star.
    — Joe Pasternak of Esther Williams

There are two good reasons why men will go to see her.
    — Howard Hughes of Jane Russell

Two profiles pasted together.
    — Dorothy Parker of Basil Rathbone

His tragedy is that of the innovator who has run out of innovations.
    — Andrew Sarris of Rouben Mamoulian

She thinks she doesn't get old. She told me once it was her cameraman who was getting older. She wanted me to fire him.
    — Joe Pasternak of Doris Day

The only way to make a film with him is to let him direct, write and produce it as well as star in it.
    — Charles Feldman of Peter Sellers

He's the fellow who, when Esther Williams jumps into the pool, gets splashed.
    — Ed Wynn of Keenan Wynn

Let's face it, Billy Wilder at work is two people — Mr Hyde and Mr Hyde.
    — Harry Kurnitz

The only Greek tragedy I know is Spyros Skouras.
    — Billy Wilder

She looked as though butter wouldn't melt in her mouth — or anywhere else.
    — Elsa Lanchester of Maureen O'Hara

Questions

Quiz

Who asked these questions, of whom, in which films?

1 George, didn't you ever want to know what's on the other side of the mountain?
2 How will you eat, through a tube?
3 Would you like a leg or a breast?
4 Do you believe the dead come back to watch the living?
5 Has Michael Finn been in today?
6 Is my aunt Minnie in there?
7 Hey, old man, you home tonight?
8 Where's the rest of me?
9 Why don't you get a divorce and settle down?
10 Got your clock?
11 What other hobbies you got?
12 What seems to be the trouble, Captain?
13 If it be a natural thing, where do it come from? Where do it go?
14 What's the bleeding time?
15 What's the going price on integrity this week?
16 She cut off her nipples with garden shears. You call that normal?
17 Does that mean, sir, that I shall not be able to play for the Old Boys?
18 Why don't you slip out of these wet clothes and into a dry martini?
19 You gentlemen aren't *really* trying to kill my son, are you?
20 Did you ever have the feeling that you wanted to go, and still have the feeling that you wanted to stay?

1 Ronald Colman to John Howard in *Lost Horizon* (1937).

2 Groucho Marx to Margaret Dumont in *At the Circus* (1939). She has just been making seating arrangements for dinner: 'You will sit upon my left hand, and you will sit upon my right hand...'

3 Grace Kelly to Cary Grant in *To Catch a Thief* (1955). They are picnicking, and she is supposedly offering him chicken, but there are other implications.

4 Judith Anderson to Joan Fontaine in *Rebecca* (1940). Sinister housekeeper Mrs Danvers is provoking the second Mrs de Winter to suicide.

5 W. C. Fields to Shemp Howard in *The Bank Dick* (1941). Mr Howard plays the proprietor of the Black Pussy Cat Cafe, and Mr Fields is prompting him to prepare a Mickey Finn for his guest.

6 The unidentified actress who pokes her nose into the famous cabin scene in *A Night at the Opera* (1935), and is promptly lost in the melee.

7 Paul Newman praying to God in *Cool Hand Luke* (1967) (which has been taken as an allegory of the crucifixion, with Newman as Christ).

8 Ronald Reagan to Ann Sheridan in *Kings Row* (1941), on waking to find that his legs have been amputated.

9 Oscar Levant to Joan Crawford in *Humoresque* (1944). Mr Levant, as usual, wrote his own lines.

10 Moore Marriott to Will Hay in *Oh Mr Porter* (1937). Hay as a seedy stationmaster has just arrived at his new post, an Irish hamlet which has lately lost a remarkable number of stationmasters. His aged dogsbody refers to the presentation clock which they all bring from their last assignment; he now has quite a collection.

11 Groucho Marx to Henry Armetta in *The Big Store* (1941). Groucho has been sleeping in the bedding department, and wakes to find himself being looked over by an Italian with a score of children.

12 Mildred Natwick to Edmund Gwenn in *The Trouble with Harry* (1955). As the Captain is tugging a dead body through the bushes, this inquiry perfectly sets a tone for the black comedy which follows.

13 Herbert Lomas to Arthur Askey in *The Ghost Train* (1941). The ghoulish stationmaster has been regaling the stranded passengers with a ghostly yarn. (There were previous versions with other actors.)

14 James Robertson Justice (irascible surgeon) to Dirk Bogarde (callow student) in *Doctor in the House* (1952). The required answer is the time it takes for bleeding to stop, but the student has not been listening and takes the remark for an oath, replying: 'Half-past two, sir...'

15 Orson Welles to Oliver Reed in *I'll Never Forget Whatshisname* (1967).

16 Elizabeth Taylor to Marlon Brando, of Julie Harris, in *Reflections in a Golden Eye* (1968).

17 Ivor Novello (schoolboy) to Ben Webster (headmaster) in Alfred Hitchcock's *Downhill* (1926). The boy has just been expelled. (The film being silent, this quotation is a sub-title.)

18 Robert Benchley to Ginger Rogers in *The Major and the Minor* (1942).

19 Jessie Royce Landis to assorted villains in an elevator in *North by Northwest* (1959).

20 The opening of Jimmy Durante's song at the piano to a delighted Monty Woolley in *The Man Who Came to Dinner* (1941).

Remakes

Quiz
Name the originals of which these were remakes:

1 *Rock A Bye Baby*
2 *Barricade*
3 *The King and I*
4 *His Girl Friday*
5 *Satan Met a Lady*
6 *The Wagons Roll at Night*
7 *On the Riviera*
8 *An Affair to Remember*
9 *Move Over Darling*
10 *High Society*
11 *Silk Stockings*
12 *The Birds and the Bees*
13 *Stage Struck*
14 *One Hour With You*
15 *Living It Up*
16 *Stolen Hours*
17 *Easy to Wed*
18 *The Strawberry Blonde*
19 *Stop! You're Killing Me*
20 *House of Wax*
21 *The Long Night*
22 *The Unfinished Dance*
23 *The Opposite Sex*
24 *Storm over the Nile*

Answers

1 *The Miracle of Morgans Creek*
2 *The Sea Wolf*
3 *Anna and the King of Siam*
4 *The Front Page*
5 *The Maltese Falcon* (first made 1931)
6 *Kid Galahad*
7 *That Night in Rio*
8 *Love Affair*
9 *My Favourite Wife*
10 *The Philadelphia Story*
11 *Ninotchka*
12 *The Lady Eve*
13 *Morning Glory*
14 *The Marriage Circle*
15 *Nothing Sacred*
16 *Dark Victory*
17 *Libelled Lady*
18 *One Sunday Afternoon*
19 *A Slight Case of Murder*
20 *The Mystery of the Wax Museum*
21 *Le Jour se Lève*
22 *Le Mort du Cygne*
23 *The Women*
24 *The Four Feathers*

Romance

Can you name the romantic actors who spoke these lines, and the films in which they did so?

1 I cannot live without my life…I cannot love without my soul…
2 This Tartar woman is for me – and my blood says 'take her'.
3 Ah me, brown eyes!
4 I'm asking you to marry me, you little fool.
5 Come with me to the Casbah…
6 Frankly, my dear, I don't give a damn.
7 Your idea of fidelity is not having more than one man in bed at the same time.
8 It must be a wonderful supper. We may not eat it, but it must be wonderful. And waiter, you see that moon? I want to see that moon in the champagne…

And what ladies took the initiative in these terms?
9 The arrangement of the features of your face is not entirely repulsive to me.
10 I wouldn't take you if you were covered in diamonds – upside down!
11 Call me sausage…
12 If you want anything, just whistle…
13 Oh Jerry, don't let's ask for the moon. We have the stars…
14 It's even better when you help.
15 I never dreamed that any mere physical experience could be so stimulating…

156

1 Laurence Olivier as Heathcliff, bemoaning the death of Cathy in *Wuthering Heights* (1939).
2 John Wayne of Susan Hayward in *The Conqueror* (1955).
3 Eugene Pallette to Margery Wilson in *Intolerance* (1916) (via a sub-title).
4 Laurence Olivier to Joan Fontaine in *Rebecca* (1940).
5 Popularly supposed to have been said by Charles Boyer to Hedy Lamarr in *Algiers* (1938), but in fact the line appears nowhere in the film.
6 Clark Gable to Vivien Leigh in *Gone with the Wind* (1939).
7 Dirk Bogarde to Julie Christie in *Darling* (1965).
8 Herbert Marshall, escorting Miriam Hopkins in *Trouble in Paradise* (1932).
9 Greta Garbo to Melvyn Douglas in *Ninotchka* (1939).
10 Joan Crawford to Jeff Chandler in *The Female on the Beach* (1955).
11 Joyce Grenfell to Lloyd Lamble in *Blue Murder at St Trinian's* (1952).
12 Lauren Bacall to Humphrey Bogart in *To Have and Have Not* (1944).
13 Bette Davis to Paul Henried in *Now Voyager* (1942).
14 Again, Bacall to Bogart in *To Have and Have Not* (1944). demonstrating the art of kissing.
15 Katharine Hepburn to Humphrey Bogart in *The African Queen* (1951) – but in fact she is referring to their descent of the rapids.

Self
Analysis

What well-known film people spoke of themselves in the following terms? (We're sure that in some cases they didn't mean it.)

1 I like to be introduced as America's foremost actor. It saves the necessity of further effort.
2 I'm as pure as the driven slush.
3 People don't know my real self and they're not about to find out.
4 Honestly, I think I've stretched a talent which is so thin it's almost opaque over a quite unbelievable term of years.
5 I may not have come up the hard way, but I have come up the whole way.
6 It's no use asking me to talk about art.
7 Everyone tells me I've had such an interesting life, but sometimes I think it's been nothing but stomach disturbances and self-concern.
8 The way life looks in my pictures is the way I want life to be.
9 A girl is…a girl. It's nice to be told you're successful at it.
10 For me the best drama is one that deals with a man in danger.
11 I am a wife-made man.
12 If I had the dough, I'd buy up the negative of every film I ever made…and start one hell of a fire.
13 I have a face like the behind of an elephant.
14 I've always found insects exciting.
15 I always wait for *The Times* each morning. I look at the obituary column, and if I'm not in it I go to work.
16 I have a child and I made a few people happy. That is all.
17 I guess my face is still the same, and so is the dialogue. Only the horses have changed.

18 My personality is that of the egotistical adventurer.

19 I've been around so long I can remember Doris Day before she was a virgin.

20 Some people have youth, some have beauty – I have menace.

21 I care nothing about the story, only how it is photographed and presented.

22 I hope the money men don't find out that I'd pay them to let me do this.

23 I want to go on until they have to shoot me.

24 I don't pretend to be an ordinary housewife.

25 I have eyes like those of a dead pig.

26 Anyone who works is a fool. I don't work – I merely inflict myself on the public.

27 He's a very very bad actor but he absolutely loves doing it.

28 I've never had a goddam artistic problem in my life, never, and I've worked with the best of them. John Ford isn't exactly a bum, is he? Yet he never gave me any manure about art.

29 I don't even notice competition. I'm a centre forward. I don't watch them. Let them watch me.

30 No one has ever discovered the truth about me – not even myself.

31 In some situations I was difficult, in odd moments impossible, in rare moments loathsome, but, at my best, unapproachably great.

32 I wouldn't act a role if it was not felt as dominating the whole story.

1 John Barrymore
2 Tallulah Bankhead
3 Yul Brynner
4 Bing Crosby
5 Bryan Forbes
6 John Ford
7 Cary Grant
8 Ross Hunter
9 Rita Hayworth
10 Howard Hawks
11 Danny Kaye
12 Sterling Hayden
13 Charles Laughton
14 Luis Bunuel
15 A. E. Matthews
16 Marlene Dietrich
17 Audie Murphy (at 40)
18 Orson Welles
19 Groucho Marx
20 Edward G. Robinson
21 Josef Von Sternberg
22 David Lean
23 Barbara Stanwyck
24 Elizabeth Taylor
25 Marlon Brando
26 Robert Morley
27 David Niven (of himself)
28 John Wayne
29 Nicol Williamson
30 'Prince' Michael Romanoff
31 Oscar Levant
32 Orson Welles

David
O. Selznick (1902-65)

Selznick was the mogul who gave up at his peak. He said in retirement:

> *Very few people have mastered the art of enjoying their wealth. I have mastered the art, and therefore I spend my time enjoying myself.*

This was not unexpected behaviour from the man who once said:

> *I don't want to be normal. Who wants to be normal?*

Yet his own memorable utterances were few, and on the sad side. He said of Hollywood:

> *Once photographed, life here is ended.*

And of the house which is so central to *Gone With the Wind*:

> *It's somehow symbolic of Hollywood that Tara was just a facade, with no rooms inside.*

An unhumorous man, intense and thorough to a fault, he was a hard taskmaster. Nunnally Johnson demurred at working for him:

> *I understand that an assignment with you consists of three months' work and six months' recuperation.*

His creative impulse surged through his internal memos, the length of which was legendary. Alfred Hitchcock said in 1965:

When I came to America twenty-five years ago to direct Rebecca, *David Selznick sent me a memo. (Pause.) I've just finished reading it. (Pause.) I think I may turn it into a motion picture. (Pause.) I plan to call it* The Longest Story Ever Told.

One memo which has been quoted was to director Charles Vidor, following one of protest from him:

I don't believe I've ever used such terms with you as idiotic. I may have thought *your excessive takes and angles were idiotic, but the most I've said was that they were a waste of my personal money.*

He certainly interfered:

The way I see it, my function is to be responsible for everything.

And:

The difference between me and other producers is that I am interested in the thousands and thousands of details that go into the making of a film. It is the sum total of all these things that either makes a great picture or destroys it.

His final claim was to have found a balance between God and Mammon:

I have never gone after honours instead of dollars. But I have understood the relationship between the two.

Mack
Sennett (1880-1960)

As befits the king of slapstick comedy, he was a thoughtful man.

The joke of life is the fall of dignity,

he once said. And his analysis of custard-pie throwing was perfectly expressed:

Non-anticipation on the part of the recipient of the pastry is the chief ingredient of the recipe.

He disclaimed originality:

Anyone who tells you he has invented something new is a fool or a liar or both.

He was firm in matters of taste:

We never make fun of religion, politics, race or mothers. A mother never gets hit with a custard pie. Mothers-in-law, yes. But mothers, never!

He summed up his comedy technique very simply:

It's got to move!

Slides

A feature of film-going in nickelodeon days were the decorative slides used between the brief entertainments. Here is a nostalgic selection :

Please Read the Titles to Yourself. Loud Reading Annoys Your Neighbours

Just a Moment Please While the Operator Changes Reels

If Annoyed When Here Please Tell the Management

Ladies and Gentlemen May safely visit this Theatre as no Offensive Films are ever Shown Here

We Aim to Present the Pinnacle of Motion Picture Perfection

Ladies, We Like your Hats, but Please Remove Them

You Wouldn't Spit on the Floor at Home, so Please Don't do it Here

Slogans

All kinds of claims have been made over the years for all kinds of product. Here are a few of the most memorable.

Famous Players in Famous Plays

is certainly the longest lasting, all the way from 1912. The films hardly lived up to it, any more than it was true that:

Selznick Pictures Create Happy Homes

Or that Warners fooled anybody by linking:

Good Films – Good Citizenship

Or MGM by claiming that their spur was:

Ars Gratia Artis (art for its own sake).

MGM's secondary claim:

More Stars than there are in Heaven

was simply a slight exaggeration. When talkies came in, two favourite lines were:

All Talking, All Singing, All Dancing

And, from Vitaphone:

Pictures that Talk Like Living People!

The whole industry sometimes gets together on a propaganda campaign. In the thirties, it was:

Go to a Motion Picture – and Let Yourself Go!

In the forties, simply:

Let's go to a movie!

In the fifties, in face of the arch-enemy television:

*Don't be a Living Room Captive! Go Out and See a
Great Movie!*

And a few years later:

Movies are Your Best Entertainment!

Song Titles

Quiz

A film about a songwriter usually takes as its title one of his most popular songs. Here are some titles: can you identify the composers?

1 *Till the Clouds Roll By*
2 *Night and Day*
3 *Swanee River*
4 *I'll See You in My Dreams*
5 *My Wild Irish Rose*
6 *My Gal Sal*
7 *Yankee Doodle Dandy*
8 *You Will Remember*
9 *Three Little Words*
10 *Deep in my Heart*
11 *I Wonder Who's Kissing Her Now*
12 *The Best Things in Life are Free*

And here are some song-title titles associated with performers. Which performers?

13 *Shine on Harvest Moon*
14 *After the Ball*
15 *Champagne Charlie*
16 *Love Me or Leave Me*
17 *Rose of Washington Square*
18 *With a Song in My Heart*
19 *Look for the Silver Lining*
20 *Somebody Loves Me*

1 Jerome Kern
2 Cole Porter
3 Stephen Foster
4 Gus Kahn
5 Chauncey Olcott
6 Vincent Dresser
7 George M. Cohan
8 Leslie Stuart
9 Bert Kalmar and Harry Ruby
10 Sigmund Romberg
11 Joe Howard
12 Brown, Henderson and de Sylva
13 Nora Bayes
14 Vesta Tilley
15 George Leybourne
16 Ruth Etting
17 Fanny Brice
18 Jane Froman
19 Marilyn Miller
20 Blossom Seeley

Stars

Stars may shine so brightly that they dazzle, but the glory of the movie variety is transient. Marie Dressler put it succinctly:

> *You're only as good as your last picture.*

Myron Selznick expressed the same thought:

> *Stars should get as much money as they can, while they can. They don't last long.*

An anonymous wit classically detailed the five stages in a star's life, as seen by a casting director:

1 *Who is Hugh O'Brian?*
2 *Get me Hugh O'Brian.*
3 *Get me a Hugh O'Brian type.*
4 *Get me a young Hugh O'Brian.*
5 *Who is Hugh O'Brian?*

While you're at the top, it can be pleasant. Robert Stack says:

> *If you're a star you go through the front door carrying the roses, instead of through the back door carrying the garbage.*

Gloria Swanson:

> *I have decided that while I am a star I will be every inch and every moment the star. Everyone from the studio gateman to the highest executive will know it.*

But there are drawbacks, as Marlon Brando found:

Once you are a star actor, people start asking you questions about politics, astronomy, archaeology and birth control.

Dustin Hoffman:

One thing about being successful is that I stopped being afraid of dying. Once you're a star you're dead already. You're embalmed.

Billie Burke:

By the time you get your name up in lights you have worked so hard and so long, and seen so many names go up and down, that all you can think of is: 'How can I keep it here?'

Some people find it easy, like John Wayne:

I play John Wayne in every part regardless of the character, and I've been doing okay, haven't I?

George Sanders was equally cynical:

The important thing for a star is to have an interesting face. He doesn't have to move it very much. Editing and camerawork can always produce the desired illusion that a performance is being given.

Ethel Barrymore took a different view:

To be a success an actress must have the face of Venus, the brain of Minerva, the grace of Terpsichore, the memory of Macaulay, the figure of Juno and the hide of a rhinoceros.

Katharine Hepburn put it more simply:

Show me an actress who isn't a personality and I'll show you a woman who isn't a star.

Jean Arthur found the going tough:

> *It's a strenuous job every day of your life to live up to the way you look on the screen.*

The temptation to try remains great. Director Michael Winner remarked recently:

> *Hitchcock said actors are cattle, but show me a cow who can earn one million dollars per film.*

But as Harry Cohn said:

> *After a while the stars believe their own publicity. I've never met a grateful performer in the film business.*

Likewise Sam Spiegel:

> *You make a star, you sometimes make a monster.*

So in the fifties the top stars gained control over their own careers, setting up their own independent companies. Jack Warner did not like the result:

> *In the old days you called the actor and made the deal with him. Now, they bring an army.*

At the same time, as Vincent Price noted:

> *One of the deaths of Hollywood is that they tried to make everyone look normal. Some of the actresses who are around today look and sound like my niece in Scarsdale. I love my niece in Scarsdale, but I wouldn't pay to see her act.*

People began to realize that they had been deceived by the apparent effortlessness of the old stars, who had lasted so long and given such good service. When Ronald Colman played a bit part in *Around the World in Eighty Days*, he was asked:

> *Did you really get a Cadillac for one day's work?*
> *— No, he replied — for the work of a lifetime.*

In the end, as Sam Goldwyn knew from experience of changing fashions, it is not the actors or the moguls who decide who is a star:

> *Producers don't make stars. God makes stars, and the public recognises his handiwork.*

And Ellen Terry had the simplest definition of star quality:

> *That little something extra.*

Supporting Players

Quiz

These lamentably unsung heroes and heroines all had their moments. Do you remember who, in what films:

1 Offered his guests potatoes, smoked a cigar in a tomb, and said: 'I have a rendezvous with the Duchesse de Guermantes'?

2 Was changed into a black bird, sought the truth about a criminal called Makropolos, and said: 'You will please clasp your hands behind your head'?

3 Impersonated a gorilla, was caught by his wife without his trousers, and said: 'This is the end – the absolute end'?

4 Played billiards with Barry Fitzgerald, preached hellfire in the west, and said: 'The soul – what is that? Can you hear it? Touch it? Smell it? No...'?

5 Was fired from a cannon, was lathered and shaved during a medical examination, and said: 'This shall be a gala day'?

6 Ran a hotel in Tahiti, was Danny Kaye's mother-in-law-to-be, and said: 'Tell me, have you been doing anything you shouldn't'?

7 Ran a mental home, played a leprechaun, and sang: 'For tonight we'll merry merry be' from a bottle'?

8 Relished a plate of onions, was stabbed by Countess Fosco, and said: 'No, sir, I don't think we can do business along those lines...'?

9 Fell off the top of Westminster Cathedral, was prosecuted for impersonating Santa Claus, and said: 'I have a high respect for your nerves. They are my old friends. I have heard you mention them with consideration these twenty years at least.'?

10 Served tea at Brighton, assisted Groucho Marx, and said: 'I positively swill in his ale'?

173

11 Ran a lemonade stall, followed Linda Darnell and, as a bartender, said: 'Sir, you rouse the artist in me'?

12 Was jealous of Maurice Chevalier, got the better of Lewis Stone, and said: 'Peace – it's wonderful!'?

13 Spied on 92nd Street, solved the mystery of Manderley, and said: 'Never thought I'd make it. Getting too old for this kind of work'?

14 Hunted the Frankenstein monster, played a butler named Barrymore, and said: 'I'd get an irrigation ditch so squirmin' full of repented sinners I pretty near drowned half of 'em!'?

15 Murdered Joan Blondell, advised Queen Victoria, and said: 'We rule with moderate strictness, and in return are satisfied with moderate obedience'?

16 Played John Brown twice, Black Michael once, and said: 'All the universe, or nothing: Which shall it be?'

1 Ernest Thesiger: *The Old Dark House, Bride of Franken-stein, Father Brown*
2 Peter Lorre: *The Raven, The Mask of Dimitrios, The Maltese Falcon*
3 Mischa Auer: *My Man Godfrey, Destry Rides Again, Lady in the Dark*
4 Walter Huston: *And then there were None, Duel in the Sun, All that Money Can Buy*
5 Margaret Dumont: *At the Circus, A Day at the Races, Duck Soup*
6 Florence Bates: *The Moon and Sixpence, The Secret Life of Walter Mitty, Rebecca*
7 Cecil Kellaway: *Harvey, The Luck of the Irish, I Married a Witch*
8 Sidney Greenstreet: *They Died with their Boots On, The Woman in White, The Maltese Falcon*
9 Edmund Gwenn: *Foreign Correspondent, Miracle on 34th Street, Pride and Prejudice*
10 Eric Blore: *The Gay Divorcee, Love Happy, Sullivan's Travels*
11 Edgar Kennedy: *Duck Soup, Unfaithfully Yours, Mad Wednesday*
12 Roland Young: *One Hour with You, David Copperfield, The Philadelphia Story*
13 Leo G. Carroll: *The House on 92nd Street, Rebecca, North by Northwest.*
14 John Carradine: *Bride of Frankenstein, The Hound of the Baskervilles, The Grapes of Wrath.*
15 H. B. Warner: *Topper Returns, Victoria the Great, Lost Horizon.*
16 Raymond Massey: *Sante Fe Trail, Seven Angry Men, The Prisoner of Zenda, Things to Come.*

Talkies

The addition of sound to the movies in 1927 was ridiculed and frantically opposed; but the industry needed the fresh impetus and at great expense the revolution was achieved.

No closer approach to resurrection has ever been made by science.

said Professor M. Pupin of the American Institute of Electrical Engineers. But it was years before he could claim perfect reproduction.

The tinkle of a glass, the shot of a revolver, a footfall on a hardwood floor, and the noise of a pack of cards being shuffled, all sounded about alike.

said Gilbert Seldes in 1929. And Tallulah Bankhead complained:

They made me sound as if I'd been castrated.

Nor was the prestige of the industry helped by claims of mathematical impossibility such as:

100% talking! 100% singing! 100% dancing!

But the public forgave all: the novelty value was tremendous, even though they missed a number of favourite stars whose voices proved unsuitable. As Jack Warner said:

Men and women whose names were known throughout the land disappeared as though they had been lost at sea.

176

And Variety summed up:

Talkies didn't do more to the industry than turn it upside down, shake the entire bag of tricks from its pocket, and advance Warner Brothers from last place to first in the league.

Directed by Robert Florey
Stage play by Fred Jackson

1929

Television

Some definitions, mostly jaundiced:

The bland leading the bland.

— Anon.

Chewing gum for the eyes.

— Frank Lloyd Wright

The longest amateur night in history.

— Robert Carson

A medium, so called because it is neither rare nor well done.

— Ernie Kovacs

A twenty-one inch prison. I'm delighted with it because it used to be that films were the lowest form of art. Now we have something to look down on.

— Billy Wilder

Why should people go out and pay money to see bad films when they can stay at home and see bad television for nothing?

— Samuel Goldwyn

A TV commercial was defined as:

The opening and closing quarter-hours of a half hour show.

Though Cedric Hardwicke thought the ads were:

The last refuge of optimism in a world of gloom.

Bob Hope as so often had the last word:

The other night I saw a Road picture so cut to make room for forty-five commercials that Bing and I weren't even in it.

TELEVISION WAR

The silent battles of the next war are being fought right now...for the secret that means control of the world!

TELEVISION LOVE

See the world of tomorrow —today...with love at first sight—a thousand miles away!

"TELEVISION SPY"

The year's most amazing drama of the century's most amazing invention!

1939

Irving
Thalberg (1899-1936)

When a man dies young, he is often underestimated. Thalberg has been lucky: the reverse proved true. Head of Universal production at twenty-one and of MGM at twenty-five, his quiet efficiency and stubborn enthusiasm, coupled with his scholarly air, made him a legend even before his untimely death at thirty-seven. As early as 1925 F. L. Collins wrote:

> *Wherever Thalberg sits is always the head of the table.*

He had apparently high aims:

> *I believe that although the motion picture may not live forever as a work of art, except in a few instances, it will be the most efficient way of showing posterity how we live now.*

He was modest enough to keep his name off the credits of his films:

> *If you are in a position to give credit, you don't need it.*

Charles MacArthur said:

> *Entertainment is Thalberg's God. He's content to serve Him without billing, like a priest at an altar or a rabbi under the scrolls.*

He was a shrewd film-maker:

> *Movies aren't made, they're remade.*

And he always had an eye for the box office. His idea of a good tag-line was:

> *Ladies, have you had a good cry lately? See* Imitation of Life *and cry unashamedly.*

And he once said to Cedric Hardwicke:

> *We should all make a killing in this business: there's so much money in the pot.*

Title Quotations

Quiz
Many film titles, especially those based on famous books, consist of quotations which may or may not be satisfactorily explained within the film. Can you name the literary source of the following?

1 *The Seventh Seal*
2 *The Root of All Evil*
3 *North by Northwest*
4 *Bullets or Ballots*
5 *The Sun Never Sets*
6 *Ill Met by Moonlight*
7 *The Sound of Music*
8 *The Voice of the Turtle*
9 *Arise My Love*
10 *The Little Foxes*
11 *Our Vines have Tender Grapes*
12 *From Here to Eternity*
13 *Gone With the Wind*
14 *Behold a Pale Horse*
15 *The Grapes of Wrath*
16 *The Razor's Edge*
17 *The Painted Veil*
18 *Paths of Glory*
19 *Now Voyager*
20 *A Fool There Was*
21 *Deadlier than the Male*
22 *For Whom the Bell Tolls*
23 *Of Mice and Men*
24 *Room at the Top*
25 *So Red the Rose*

1 *The Bible:* Revelation 6.
And I saw in the right hand of him that sat on the throne a book...sealed with seven seals...

2 *The Bible:* 1 Epistle Paul 3.

The love of money is the root of all evil.

3 The leading character feigns madness, and the title seems to be a slight misquotation from Shakespeare's *Hamlet*:

I am but mad north-northwest; when the wind is southerly, I know a hawk from a handsaw.

4 Speech by Abraham Lincoln.

The ballot is stronger than the bullet.

5 Speech by Christopher North (1899).

...His Majesty's Dominions, on which the sun never sets...

6 Shakespeare, *A Midsummer Night's Dream.*

Ill met by moonlight, proud Titania.

7 Shakespeare, *The Merchant of Venice.*

How sweet the moonlight sleeps upon this bank! Here will we sit, and let the sounds of music Creep in our ears...

8, 9, 10, 11 *The Bible:* The Song of Songs.

...the time of the singing of birds is come, and the voice of the turtle is heard in our land... Arise, my love, my fair one, and come away...Take us the foxes, the little foxes, that spoil the vines... for our vines have tender grapes...

12 Rudyard Kipling, 'Gentleman Rankers'.

Gentleman rankers, out on the spree,
Damned from here to eternity.

13 Ernest Dowson, 'Cynara'.

I have forgot much, Cynara! Gone with the wind,
Flung roses, roses riotously with the throng,
Dancing, to put thy pale, lost lilies out of mind...

14 *The Bible:* Revelation 6.

And I looked, and behold a pale horse: and the
name of him that sat on him was Death.

15 Julia Ward Howe, 'The Battle Hymn of the American Republic'.

Mine eyes have seen the glory of the coming of the
Lord:
He is tramping out the vintage where the grapes of
wrath are stored.

16 Oriental proverb.

The sharp edge of a razor is difficult to pass over;
thus the wise say the path to salvation is hard.

17 Percy Bysshe Shelley, 'Sonnet'.

Lift not the painted veil which those who live
Call life...

18 Thomas Gray, 'Elegy in a Country Churchyard'.

The paths of glory lead but to the grave.

19 Walt Whitman 'Leaves of Grass'.

Now, voyager, sail thou forth to seek and find.

20 Rudyard Kipling, 'The Vampire'.

> *A fool there was, and he made his prayer...*
> *To a rag, and a bone, and a hank of hair...*

21 Rudyard Kipling, 'The Female of the Species'.

> *The female of the species is more deadly than the*
> *male...*

22 John Donne, 'Devotions'.

> *Any man's death diminishes me, because I am in-*
> *volved in mankind: therefore never send to know*
> *for whom the bell tolls: it tolls for thee.*

23 Robert Burns, 'To a Mouse'.

> *The best laid plans of mice and men*
> *Gang aft agley...*

24 Daniel Webster, on entering the overcrowded legal profession :

> *There is always room at the top.*

25 Edward Fitzgerald, 'The Rubaiyat of Omar Khayyam'.

> *I sometimes think that never blows so red*
> *The rose as where some buried Caesar bled...*

Spencer
Tracy (1900-67)

*The guy's good. There's nobody in the business who
can touch him, and you're a fool to try. And the
bastard knows it, so don't fall for that humble stuff!*

This tribute came from Clark Gable, who suffered from co-starring with Tracy in several MGM movies of the thirties. On the
other hand, Katharine Hepburn once said:

*I think Spencer always thought that acting was a
rather silly way for a man to make a living.*

She also caught his essential strength:

*He's like an old oak tree, or the summer, or the wind.
He belongs to the era when men were men.*

But Hepburn was exposed to his aggressive wit when they met
in 1941 to make *Woman of the Year*:

*I'm afraid I'm a little tall for you, Mr Tracy.
— Don't worry, I'll soon cut you down to my size.*

He ranged from supreme self-confidence to abject despair. In
1931 he complained:

*This mug of mine is as plain as a barn door. Why
should people pay thirty five cents to look at it?*

He remembered:

*There were times when my pants were so thin, I
could sit on a dime and know if it was heads or tails.*

Later he wondered at his own success:

> *The physical labour actors have to do wouldn't tax an embryo.*

Perhaps this puzzlement was responsible for his attitude to the press:

> *Write anything you want about me. Make up something. Hell, I don't care.*

But he did care, and he cared about his work. Perhaps Humphrey Bogart best summed up his appeal:

> *Spence is the best we have, because you don't see the mechanism at work.*

Trends

R. D. McCann said that in Hollywood the only familiar, solid, bedrock certainty is sudden change. That goes for the entire industry, which throughout its history has been subject to the whims of fashion and has moved in a gingerly way from one crisis to another. In the midst of such uncertainty the industry's leaders can only comfort themselves with the incontrovertible adage:

> *There's nothing wrong with this business that a few good movies can't cure.*

The trouble has been to find out what kind of movies, at any given time, are good ones in the eyes of the public. As Adolph Zukor said long ago:

> *The public is never wrong.*

And as Bryan Forbes said:

> *Nobody can be a prophet in an industry which is entirely dependent on the public whim.*

Walter Wanger knew that:

> *Nothing is as cheap as a hit, no matter how much it cost.*

Unfortunately the public has not always been in the forefront of good taste. When close-ups were first introduced, many audiences felt cheated and yelled:

> *Show us their feet!*

But without an advance in technical quality the film could hardly have survived. Billy Bitzer, the famous cameraman, said:

> *The fade-out gave us a really dignified touch – we didn't have a five cent movie anymore.*

It is true that the moguls have sometimes taken a long time to answer the public's call. Ted Willis said in 1966:

> *The film business is like that prehistoric monster the dinosaur, which apparently had two brains, one in its head and one in its rear.*

It was not always thus: in the golden years they knew a thing or two. At Warners, for instance, Bette Davis said:

> *We had the answer, the sequel and the successor to everything.*

But even imitation did not always pay. Darryl Zanuck knew:

> *Only the first picture of a cycle really succeeds: all the imitators dwindle.*

Herman Mankiewicz in 1937 was well aware of the limitations of his medium:

> *In a novel the hero can lay ten gals and marry a virgin for the finish. In a movie this is not allowed: the hero as well as the heroine has to be a virgin. The villain can lay anyone he wants, have as much fun as he likes getting rich, and cheating the servants. But you have to shoot him in the end.*

Cesare Zavattini in 1945 had a similar idea:

> *The world is full of people thinking in myths.*

Iris Barry in 1926 scorned film clichés:

Why must all American movie mothers be white-haired and tottery even though their children are mere tots? Does the menopause not operate in the U.S.?

Reality was entirely shunned. Wilson Mizner in the early talkie era commented:

The public doesn't want to know what goes on behind the scenes. It prefers to believe that a cameraman hung in the clouds, mid-Pacific, the day Barrymore fought the whale.

Samuel Goldwyn is credited with the tersest capsuling of the tradition that audiences wanted to be soothed and not stimulated:

Messages are for Western Union.

Even Terry Ramsaye, editing a trade journal in 1936, complained:

If they want to preach a sermon, let them hire a hall.

This was the day of the formula:

Boy meets girl, boy loses girl, boy gets girl.

The public paid to see it and demanded more of the same. A 1943 exhibitor said:

You could open a can of sardines and there'd be a line waiting to get in.

Momentary turns of fashion could of course be allowed for, so many movies were being made. When Variety headlined:

STICKS NIX HICK PIX

it was a simple matter to discontinue the movies about poor hillbillies to which the midwestern audiences had shown such

190

antipathy. Towards the fifties, however, there were signs of growing unease: no kind of film, and no star, could be absolutely relied on to make money. Hollywood had previously regarded the international market as a pleasant source of extra revenue; now film-making had to be geared to it. Alfred Hitchcock, however, felt that no change of style was necessary:

> *When we make films for the United States, we automatically make them for the world, for the United States is full of foreigners.*

But Hitch did note a change of emphasis:

> *In the old days, villains had moustaches and kicked the dog. Audiences are smarter today. They don't want their villain to be thrown at them with green limelight on his face. They want an ordinary human being with failings.*

The studio conveyor belt was outdated: everyone was bitten by the location bug. Rouben Mamoulian said in 1957:

> *We have forsaken the magic of the cinema. We have gotten too far away from the cinematic effects achievable by camera angles and creative editing.*

There was another increasing danger:

> *You have to offer the public something a helluva lot better than they can get for free on TV.*

What was offered was 3–D, which failed. As Hitch said:

> *A nine-days' wonder – and I came in on the ninth day.*

Then came CinemaScope and the other wide-screen processes, but the extra size only rarely contributed towards a better entertainment. Content was what mattered. The only reliable regular audience was for cheap horror films. Said Vincent Price in 1965:

The cinemas have bred a new race of giant pop-corn-eating rats.

At last the English came back into fashion as film-makers, chiefly on the strength of their actors and their 'X' subjects. This success had its drawbacks, according to Tony Garnett:

To be an Englishman in the film business is to know what it's like to be colonialised.

Sex had come to stay. Said Shelagh Delaney:

The cinema has become more and more like the theatre: it's all mauling and muttering.

Said Billy Wilder:

Titism has taken over the country. But Audrey Hepburn singlehanded may make bozooms a thing of the past. The director will not have to invent shots where the girl leans forward for a glass of scotch and soda.

Said Adolphe Menjou:

The Brando school are grabbers, not lovers. If it wasn't that the script says they get the girl, they wouldn't.

Said Bob Hope in 1968:
Last year Hollywood made the first pictures with dirty words. This year we made the pictures to go with them.

And in 1971:

The line 'I love you' is no longer a declaration but a demonstration.

In the same year Candice Bergen admitted:

I may not be a great actress but I've become the

*greatest at screen orgasms. Ten seconds of heavy
breathing, roll your head from side to side, simulate
a slight asthma attack and die a little.*

And Frank Capra snorted:

*Hollywood film-making of today is stooping to cheap
salacious pornography in a crazy bastardization of a
great art.*

The system had crumbled, the studios were empty, every movie
was a new enterprise, usually shot in some far-flung corner of
the earth. Bob Hope again, in 1968:

*This year is a good one for Hollywood. Some of the
movies nominated for Oscars were even made here.*

Hal Wallis had another complaint:

*In the old days we had the time and money to give
prospective stars a slow build-up. Today, an actor
makes it fast or he just doesn't make it at all.*

Orson Welles realised that:

*The trouble with a movie these days is that it's old
before it's released. It's no accident that it comes in a
can.*

And Billy Wilder:

*Today we spend eighty per cent of our time making
deals and twenty per cent making pictures.*

Otto Preminger remembers when:

*There were giants in the industry. Now it is an era
of midgets and conglomerates.*

The watchword for the seventies is violence. Hear the producer of *The Strawberry Statement*:

> *We live in a time when revolution is a very saleable commodity.*

Hear Roman Polanski in 1971:

> *Nothing is too shocking for me. When you tell the story of a man who loses his head, you have to show the head being cut off. Otherwise it's just a dirty joke without a punch line.*

Hear Ken Russell, middle-aged enfant terrible of the same year:

> *This is not the age of manners. This is the age of kicking people in the crotch and telling them something and getting a reaction. I want to shock people into awareness. I don't believe there's any virtue in understatement.*

Type
Casting

Some voices of despair :

I couldn't go on forever being Little Miss Fixit who burst into song.
— *Deanna Durbin*

I was a fourteen-year-old boy for thirty years.
— *Mickey Rooney*

After The Wizard of Oz *I was typecast as a lion, and there aren't all that many parts for lions.*
— *Bert Lahr*

If I made Cinderella, *the audience would be looking for the body in the coach.*
— *Alfred Hitchcock*

Aren't you tired of always playing Spencer Tracy?
— What am I supposed to do, play Bogart?
— *Spencer Tracy*

Rudolph
Valentino (1895-1926)

His acting is largely confined to protruding his large, almost occult eyes until the vast areas of white are visible, drawing back the lips of his wide, sensuous mouth to bare his gleaming teeth, and flaring his nostrils.

Thus Adolph Zukor's famous put-down; but Valentino's simple technique was very effective on female audiences the world over. Yet in the year of his death, 1926, he wrote:

A man should control his life. Mine is controlling me.

And H. L. Mencken summed him up:

He was essentially a highly respectable young man; his predicament touched me. Here was one who was catnip to women...he had youth and fame...and yet he was very unhappy.

Verse
and Worse

Can you name the films in which the following snatches of
poetry, verse or song were of significance?

1 So stand by, your glasses steady.
  The world is a world of lies.
  Here's to the dead already –
  Hurrah for the next man who dies!

2 I know a man.
  – What man?
  Man with a power.
  –What power?
  The power of voodoo.
  –Who do?
  You do.
  –Do what?
  Know a man.
  – What man?
  Man with a power...

3 They're either too young or too old.
  They're either too grey or too grassy green.
  The pickings are poor and the crop is lean.
  There isn't any gravy: the gravy's in the navy...

4 The pellet with the poison's in the chalice from the palace.
  The flagon with the dragon has the brew that is true.

5 Do not despair
  For Johnny Head-in-Air.
  He sleeps as sound
  As Johnny Underground.

197

Fetch out no shroud
For Johnny In-The-Cloud.
Best keep your head
And see his children fed.

6 Every night when the moon is bright
The miller's ghost is seen.
The mill wheel turns though the night is still...
He haunts the station, he haunts the mill
And the land that lies between...

7 I build my house of stones;
I build my house of bricks.
I have no chance to sing and dance
For work and play don't mix.

8 Some men goes for women,
And some men goes for boys;
But my love's warm and beautiful,
And makes a baa-ing noise...

9 When stars are bright
On a frosty night,
Beware thy bane
On the rocky lane...

10 When the tide runs low in the smugglers' cove
And the headless horseman rides above,
He drives along with his wild hallo,
And that's the time when the smugglers go in their little
  boats to the schooner and bring back the kegs of brandy
  and rum and put them all in the Devil's Cove below.

11 If you aint eatin' Wham
You aint eatin' ham.

12 Your wife is safe with Tonetti –
He prefers spaghetti.

1 The toast in *The Dawn Patrol.*
2 Juvenile doggerel used by Cary Grant in *The Bachelor and the Bobbysoxer* when he has to play up to Shirley Temple's crush on him.
3 Sung by Bette Davis in *Thank Your Lucky Stars,* and attacked at the time as against the best interests of wartime propaganda. The star's delivery naturally added to the disenchanted effect. One more couplet from the song:

> Tomorrow I'll go hiking with that Eagle Scout
> unless
> I get a call from Grandpa for a snappy game of
> chess...

4 The basis of a hilarious sequence in *The Court Jester.* Danny Kaye has to joust against a large and vicious opponent, and Mildred Natwick spikes one of the drinking cups. Unfortunately repetition of the couplet gets everyone confused.
5 John Pudney's famous poem written for *The Way to the Stars* in which it has been written by a squadron leader who is killed; his friend reads it to his widow.
6 For British comedy specialists! The old Irish legend in *Oh Mr Porter,* recited by the toothless Harbottle.
7 Sung by the third of Disney's *Three Little Pigs.*
8 Sung by the public house drunks in *Straw Dogs.*
9 For film buffs only! The family curse of the Hammonds in *The Undying Monster* (1942).
10 Another Will Hay comedy, *Ask a Policeman* (1939). This insane piece of doggerel, remembered by aged Moore Mariot's even more aged father, provides a clue to and a cover for the activities of the criminals.
11 The slogan which eluded ad man Cary Grant all through *Mr Blandings Builds his Dream House* finally dropped casually from the lips of his black cook.
12 Erik Rhodes as the professional co-respondent in *The Gay Divorce.*

Orson
Welles (1915-   )

There, but for the grace of God, goes God.

So snapped Herman Mankiewicz during the making of *Citizen Kane*. There must have been something infuriatingly godlike about Orson the young Messiah from New York, brought out with his troupe to play with what he called:

The biggest toy train set any boy ever had.

Unfortunately, as he later admitted,

I started at the top and worked down.

It was indeed the only way to go: he could not, either by temperament or ability, make the films Hollywood wanted. The end of his reign came when:

They let the studio janitor cut The Magnificent Ambersons *in my absence.*

The years that followed saw an amassment of unfinished projects and haphazard wanderings over Europe, with flashes of acting genius in between. Paul Holt called him:

The oldest enfant terrible in the world.

Jean Cocteau saw him as:

An active loafer, a wise madman.

Ken Tynan called him:

A superb bravura director, a fair bravura producer,

*and a limited bravura writer; but an incomparable
bravura personality.*

Perhaps he best summed up his own career:

> *Everybody denies I am a genius — but nobody ever
> called me one!*

Mae
West (1892-   )

Whole books of Mae West's wit have been published. A much cleverer woman than she is usually given credit for being, she seems to talk in epigrams. In her seventies on TV, when someone gushed:

Oh, Miss West, I've heard so much about you

the reply was:

Yeah, but you can't prove a thing.

When a life jacket was named after her during World War II, her reaction had the appearance of spontaneity:

I've been in Who's Who *and I know what's what, but it's the first time I ever made the dictionary.*

However, she never did say:

Come up and see me sometime...

At least, not quite, and not in the film she was supposed to. She did however say:

Beaulah, peel me a grape.

which for some reason has passed into the language. Her first screen appearance is also legendary:

Goodness, what beautiful diamonds!
— Goodness had nothing to do with it, dearie.

For the rest, one can only list a few sparklers:

*She's one of the finest women who ever walked the
streets.*

*It's not the men in my life, it's the life in my men
that counts.*

I wouldn't let him touch me with a ten foot pole.

How tall are you, son?
— Ma'am, I'm six feet seven inches.
*Let's forget the six feet and talk about the seven
inches.*

(On arriving at her office and being greeted by a score of virile
young men)

*I'm feeling a little tired today. One of those fellows'll
have to go home.*

(In a Broadway costume play, when the romantic lead got his
sword so tangled in his braid that it stuck up at an unfortunate
angle)

Is that your sword, or are you just pleased to see me?

I wouldn't even lift my veil for that guy.

*When I'm good I'm very good, but when I'm bad
I'm better.*

*It isn't what I do, but how I do it. It isn't what I say,
but how I say it. And how I look when I do it and
say it.*

(On the mirrored ceiling over her bed)

I like to know what I'm doing.

*Whenever I'm caught between two evils, I take the
one I've never tried.*

Small wonder that her first co-star, George Raft, remarked of her debut:

She stole everything but the cameras.

In a non-permissive age, she made remarkable inroads against the taboos of her day, and did so without even lowering her neckline. Indeed, her most effective moment may have been in a scene in which she drove a funfair crowd wild with a dance that did nothing but tease. As she disappears into the tent, she wraps up years of experience, enjoyment and disapproval of the sex war into one word:

Suckers!

1932

Who
Said That?

Quiz
Most film buffs will have heard the following lines. But who said them, in what circumstances? In films, or in reality?

1 Can you imagine being wonderfully overpaid for dressing up and playing games?
2 Bring on the empty horses!
3 So they call me Concentration Camp Erhardt?
4 I'm not happy. I'm not happy at all.
5 Life's never quite interesting enough, somehow. You people who come to the movies know that.
6 I'm terrified of policemen.
7 Oh, Victor, please don't go to the underground meeting tonight...
8 The trouble is that you are only interested in art, and I am only interested in money.
9 Yonda is the castle of my fodda...
10 Son, always give 'em a good show, and travel first class.
11 This is really just a very simple engineering problem...
12 No mean Machiavelli is smiling, cynical Sidney Kidd.
13 It's the only disease you don't look forward to being cured of.
14 You understand that last night was only a comedy.
15 Move those ten thousand horses a little to the right.
16 I have lived in the theatre as a trappist monk lives in his faith.
17 Paint it!
18 *L'oiseau chante avec ses doigts...*
19 The lunatics have taken over the asylum.
20 Boys, I've an idea. Let's fill the screen with tits.
21 There can only be one winner, folks, but isn't that the American way?
22 Hush up, telephone – I's a-comin', I's a-comin'!

1 David Niven describing his profession in interview.
2 Director Michael Curtiz, whose command of English was somewhat haphazard, is alleged to have issued this instruction during the location filming of *The Charge of the Light Brigade* (1936).
3 An oft-repeated line (by Sig Ruman and Jack Benny) in Lubitsch's *To Be or Not To Be* (1942).
4 Walter Abel as the harrassed editor in Wilder's *Arise My Love* (1940). The line became something of a catch phrase in the forties.
5 Shirley Booth's introduction to *The Matchmaker* (1957).
6 Alfred Hitchcock, invariably, when asked what, if anything, scares him.
7 Ingrid Bergman to Paul Henried in *Casablanca* (1942).
8 Bernard Shaw, allegedly, to Samuel Goldwyn when they were trying to negotiate terms for the filming of Shaw's plays.
9 Tony Curtis in *The Black Shield of Falworth* (1954). His Brooklyn accent was derided: he was playing an English nobleman.
10 Walter Huston's advice to his son John.
11 Howard Hughes, designing a bra for his star Jane Russell in *The Outlaw* (1943).
12 Cary Grant to James Stewart (speaking about Henry Daniell) in *The Philadelphia Story* (1940).
13 Everett Sloane speaking of old age in *Citizen Kane* (1941).
14 From the suicide note of Jean Harlow's husband, Paul Bern. What he meant has never been ascertained.
15 An instruction from D. W. Griffith during the filming of *The Birth of a Nation* (1915).
16 George Sanders as Addison de Witt in *All About Eve* (1950).
17 Howard Hughes' only instruction to the staff of RKO Studios which he had just acquired.
18 The wireless message from the other world in *Orphee* (1949).
19 A comment by Richard Rowland of Metro when United Artists was taken over by Chaplin, Pickford, Fairbanks and Griffith.

20 Hunt Stromberg on taking over the production of Flaherty's *White Shadows in the South Seas* (1928).
21 Gig Young as MC of the marathon dance contest in *They Shoot Horses, Don't They?* (1970).
22 Hattie McDaniel as the black mammy in *The Great Lie* (1941).

It Brings the Panther Woman to the Screen!

H. G. WELLS
ISLAND OF LOST SOULS
WITH
**CHARLES LAUGHTON
BELA LUGOSI
RICHARD ARLEN
LEILA HYAMS**
AND THE
PANTHER WOMAN
A Paramount Picture

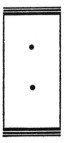

1933

Billy
Wilder (1906-   )

The pixie wit of this Hollywood Viennese has sporadically
brightened the film scene for more than thirty years. Nor does
he save all his wit for his scripts: he is the most quotable of
film-makers:

> *I have ten commandments. The first nine are, thou
> shalt not bore. The tenth is, thou shalt have right of
> final cut.*

On critical prejudice:

> *What critics call dirty in our movies, they call lusty
> in foreign films.*

On fashion:

> *You watch, the new wave will discover the slow dis-
> solve in ten years or so.*

On messages:

> *In certain pictures I do hope they will leave the*
>
> *cinema a little enriched, but I don't make them pay
> a buck and a half and then ram a lecture down their
> throats.*

On direction:

> *The best directing is the one you don't see.*

On technique:

> *The close-up is such a valuable thing – like a trump
> at bridge.*

A man with such waspish wit naturally invites retaliation, even from his wife :

> *Long before Billy Wilder was Billy Wilder, he thought he was Billy Wilder.*

That may have been in response to a cable he sent her from Paris just after the war. She had requested him to buy and send a bidet. After a vain search he sent the message:

> *Unable obtain bidet. Suggest handstand in shower.*

Wilder is the kind of man who can scarcely observe anything without being funny about it. For instance:

> *France is a country where the money falls apart in your hands and you can't tear the toilet paper.*

Michael
Winner (1935-)

In a time when diffidence is fashionable, it is refreshing to find a young British director who seems deliberately to court comparison with Erich Von Stroheim:

A team effort is a lot of people doing what I say.

Original? It seems so. It is also true; and unlike Von Stroheim Mr Winner does get his films out on time and below budget, facts which tend to atone for his arrogance. He knows that:

In this business, disaster is always just around the corner.

He remembers the days when:

You could make a film for £100,000 and get your money back from people sheltering from the rain.

He won't make the mistake of imagining that those days are still here. He enjoys the big money:

Success has gone to my stomach.

And he finds that:

The hardest part of directing is staying awake for nine weeks at a stretch.

Writers

Writers have traditionally been undervalued in Hollywood. Ernst Lubitsch said:

> *In this town we acquire the finest novels in order to smell the leather bindings.*

Graham Greene put the same thought a different way when he commented on the film version of his novel *Stamboul Train* (they even changed the title to *Orient Express*):

> *If there was any truth in the original it had been carefully altered. If anything had been left unchanged it was because it was untrue.*

Joseph L. Mankiewicz was similarly bitter:

> *I felt the urge to direct because I couldn't stomach what was being done with what I wrote.*

He never lost his conviction of the writer's supreme importance:

> *Every screenwriter worthy of the name has already directed his film when he has written his script.*

And:

> *I write plays for the screen...I write essentially for audiences who come to listen to a film as well as look at it.*

There has been plenty of reason for cynicism. An anonymous wit once remarked:

211

> *Hollywood buys stories when they are topical and screens them when they are typical.*

Another anonymous story has been passed down about Ben Hecht and Charles MacArthur's script for *Wuthering Heights*:

> *They did it in two weeks flat. They didn't bother too much about the Brontë book: they did it from an outline.*

Most of the bosses felt the same way. Jack Warner confessed in his autobiography:

> *I would rather take a fifty-mile hike than crawl through a book. I prefer to skip the long ones and get a synopsis from the story department.*

Darryl F.
Zanuck (1902-   )

The hardiest and longest-lived of the moguls of Hollywood's golden age was somehow the most disappointing in terms of colour and personality. His most personal trait is his allegedly avid sexual appetite, though he has himself said :

> *Any of my indiscretions were with people, not actresses.*

He is a tough employer:

> *There was only one boss I believed in, and that was me.*

As his biographer Mel Gussow said:

> *He couldn't stand stubbornness in anybody but himself.*

Zanuck's most famous bon mot was addressed to a minion too eager to please:

> *For God's sake don't say yes until I finish talking!*

He spent thirty-five years, more or less, as boss of Twentieth Century Fox, and before that for ten years was production head of Warners. His ideas for remakes were legendary:

> *I want to do* Air Force *in a submarine.*

Another of his credos is now outdated:

> *When you get a sex story in biblical garb, you can open your own mint.*

He produced many worthy films, perhaps for rather stodgy reasons:

> *We are in the business primarily to provide enter-tainment, but in doing so we do not dodge the issue if we can also provide enlightenment.*

Or, more pithily:

> *I know audiences feed on crap, but I cannot believe we are so lacking that we cannot dish it up to them with some trace of originality.*

On another occasion however he was optimistic:

> *Public taste is an ascending spiral.*

But his final production philosophy was:

> *Take a chance and spend a million dollars and hope you're right.*

Last
Round Up

A few favourite unclassifiable moments.

Bette Davis, on having pointed out to her a starlet who had allegedly slept her way to the top:

I see – she's the original good time that was had by all.

Billy Wilder to his cinematographer during the filming of *Sunset Boulevard*:

Johnny, keep it out of focus. I want to win the foreign picture award.

An anonymous wartime crack:

In case of an air raid, go directly to RKO: they haven't had a hit in years.

Will Rogers, philosophizing:

What's the salvation of the movies? I say, run 'em backwards. It can't hurt, and it's worth a trial.

King Vidor, evaluating one of his own movies:

The picture was so bad they had to do retakes before they could put it on the shelf.

Carole Lombard, refusing a role in an Orson Welles film:

I can't win working with Welles. If the picture's a

*hit he will get the credit, and if it's a flop, I'll be
blamed.*

Katharine Hepburn, analysing the mystique of Fred Astaire
and Ginger Rogers:

He gives her class and she gives him sex.

John Grierson, evaluating the decline of Josef Von Sternberg:

When a director dies, he becomes a photographer.

Sir Cedric Hardwicke on judgement by sneak preview:

*On Hollywood's theory that the audience knows
best, the schoolboy's 'lousy' becomes the last word
in dramatic criticism.*

Jean Renoir, leaving Hollywood after an enforced wartime
sojourn:

*Goodbye, Mr Zanuck: it certainly has been a
pleasure working at 16th Century Fox.*

Louis B. Mayer on the product of his own studios:

Beautiful pictures for beautiful people.

Jesse L. Lasky on being a producer:

*The producer must be a prophet and a general, a
diplomat and a peacemaker, a miser and a spend-
thrift. He must have vision tempered by hindsight,
daring governed by caution, the patience of a saint
and the iron of a Cromwell.*

Adolph Zukor taking responsibility for his company's product:

Fish stinks from the head.

The same Mr Zukor explaining his first explanation into film-making:

I was struck by the moral potentialities of the screen.

Child actress Margaret O'Brien, taking instruction in a tearful scene:

When I cry, do you want the tears to run all the way, or shall I stop halfway down?

Howard Hawks, commenting on his penchant for remaking films with similar characters and situations:

When you find out a thing goes pretty well, you might as well do it again.

Victor Mature, when Rita Hayworth deserted him for Orson Welles, with whom she had been working in a charity magic act:

Apparently the way to a girl's heart is to saw her in half.

Walter Wanger on Hollywood gossip columnists:

This is the only industry that finances its own blackmail.

Allan Dwan on survival in Hollywood:

If you get your head up above the mob, they try to knock it off. If you stay down, you last forever.

Richard Brooks on the great Hollywood moguls:

They were monsters and pirates and bastards right down to the bottom of their feet but they loved movies. Some of the jerks running the business today don't even have faces.

217

Robert Lord on the film city:

> *It's such nonsense, this immorality of Hollywood.*
> *We're all too tired.*

Robert Benchley after viewing an arty film:

> *There's less in this than meets the eye.*

And Spencer Tracy, on finding himself working for a director with 'artistic' ideas who tried to turn every gesture into a symbol:

> *I'm too tired and old and rich for all this, so let's do the scene.*

Two cables. The first from Laurence Olivier to Richard Burton during the publicity fracas while *Cleopatra* was shooting:

> *Make up your mind, dear heart. Do you want to be a great actor or a household word?*

Burton allegedly replied:

> *Both.*

The other cable is from a British publicist who wired Cary Grant's agent:

> *How old Cary Grant?*

The wire accidentally reached Mr Grant himself, who cheerily wired back:

> *Old Cary Grant fine. How you?*

A final thought from Auguste Lumiere, pioneer of cinematography, in 1895:

> *Young man, you can be grateful that my invention is not for sale, for it would undoubtedly ruin you. It can be exploited for a certain time as a scientific curiosity, but apart from that it has no commercial value whatsoever.*

Index of Quoters
and Quoted

This index includes those who made the quoted remarks and all those about whom remarks were made. It does not include actors who are mentioned within the quizzes as having delivered the lines in films.

220